ADVENTURES OF A SNAKE HUNTER

By Frank Weed

Copyright 2019 by Frank Weed

Published by Southern Chick Lit

All rights reserved. No part of this publication may be reproduced, distributed, or transmitted in any form or by any means, including photocopying, recording, or any other electronic or mechanical methods without the prior written permission of the publisher, except in the case of brief quotations embodied in critical reviews and certain other non-commercial uses by copyright law.

Photos provided by Frank Weed, Tommy Taylor, John Kenmitzer, Steve Handley.

Other Books by Frank Weed

Gone Snake Hunting

Table of Contents

In The Beginning 10
My First Snakes 15
Old Snake Lover? 18
Hooked on Snakes 20
Turtles 23
Lion 27
Snakes in the Walls 29
Pet Python 31
Goldfish 33
The Cross-Eyed Rattler 35
Gator in the Pool 37
Miss Vermont 39
South American Rodeo 41
Ross Heilman - Stage Name, Kananga 43
Arthur Jones 48
Gator Needed in Oklahoma 51
Snake Lecture 55
Learning the Tricks of the Trade 57
Fort Matanzas Rattlers 59
A Smart Rattler 62
Bugs, Spiders and Snakes for Sale 64
Snake Bites 67

Scarlet Kingsnakes 77

Road Hunting Tricks 80

Lots of Water Snakes.. 82

Route 27 85

Robbers 88

Tarzan 91

No Trick 93

A Mud Snake Bonanza 95

More Garter Snakes 97

Too Close Alligator 98

Gordon Johnston 101

A Cold Piece of Tin 104

State Road 27 106

A Snake Lover He Wasn't 108

Four-Lined Skinks.. 109

Australian Pine Trees and Yellow Rats.. 111

Pop Top King Snake 114

Wasps 115

Dragline Indigo... 117

The Knack or Lack of Knack 118

$$$$$$$ 120

Caiman Catching 121

Problem Gator 124

Cold Rattlers 125

Look Before You Volunteer 127

Billboards	129
Spiders, Lizards and Tree Frogs	132
Good Eyes	133
Cottonmouths Galore	136
A Snake Falls in My Hand	138
Big Cottonmouth	141
Guard Rails and Railroad Ties	143
Fort Lauderdale Crocodile	145
Monkey Business	149
Crocs in the Mangroves	151
Jamaica Wreck	153
Gators for a Croc	155
Fresh Water Shrimp	157
A Croc Scare	159
Airport Crocodiles	160
Jamaican Boas	162
Just Another Jamaican Croc	165
A Long, Long Ride	166
Tarantulas	174
Goins King	177
A Texas Ranch Hunt	179
Lizards	182
Two Quick Westerns	184
Worm Snakes	186
Mexican Milksnakes	189

The Joy of Road Hunting 191

Lose some 194

Blair's King Snakes in Texas 197

Texas Flood 200

Rattlesnake 203

White Lie 204

Hardeeville Reds 206

Feisty Copperhead 208

Claxton Rattlesnake Roundup 210

Bill Tudor 213

It's Great To Be Young 216

Hay, Piles, and Burns 219

You Can't Catch Them All 221

Frank Over the Years 224

Pinned Down by a Sign 231

Strange Bedfellows 232

Three Kings 234

A Smart Bird 235

Croc Catching 236

In The Movies 239

Rattlers with Personalities 242

Bruce Bednar 245

Morris 246

Lobo 248

Wildlife Officer 249

Snakeskin Stuff 251

Wiggly 253

Mom 255

Allen 256

Every Day Is Different 258

Dangerous Deer 260

Good Boy and Company 263

Turner River Road 266

Snakes Are Where You Find Them 269

Waltzing Bear 271

Alley the Gator 273

A Few Fish Stories 275

Mouse in the Blouse 279

The Voice — My Guardian Angel 282

Dinosaur Tracks and Fossilized Bones 284

Sixth Sense 287

ZZ TOP 289

Diamondbacks and Pigmys 291

Pigmys at Dusk 292

Recent Happenings 293

Watch Your Step 295

More About Frank Weed 297

Dedication

To my parents who started my love for all things in nature.

In The Beginning

Back before the Florida construction craze started and just as tourists were beginning to travel to Florida, Frank Weed along with his parents Frank and Ellen helped to develop what has become known as eco-tourism. They, along with other famous herpetologists, alligator wrestlers, and other wildlife handlers, introduced Florida's wildlife to people throughout the United States in animal shows, lectures, photo shoots, and magazine articles. They stressed the importance of keeping eco-systems pure and natural.

The Weeds were breeders of big cats in the 1950's. 60's,70's and 80's. Where did they breed? In the Everglades on their compound. World famous wildlife photographers could be found there taking photos of the pumas, cougars, alligators, opossums, raccoons, poisonous snakes, and more for publication in various sports and hunting magazines.

Frank followed in his parents' footsteps, sharing his love of the outdoors and animals, particularly snakes, with others. Frank has been a naturalist since the time he could walk and enjoys showing and educating others about wildlife, particularly snakes, and their importance to the natural habitat of Florida.

All of the following stories are true and gives you an idea of what it was like to grow up with famous parents, big name friends who were on the forefront of introducing the public to Florida wildlife, and how it all came about.

Here's Frank's *Adventures of a Snake Hunter*. Enjoy!

Ellen & Frank Weed

Frank and Python

April 11, 2019

Dear Readers:

Some of these stories have been previously published and have been updated. New photos are also included.

To walk out in the fields or woods find a snake, pick it up and put it in a bag and carry it home, that isn't much of a story. I've done that hundreds of times, but every once in a while, something exciting or really bizarre happens and that makes it memorable. That's what these stones are all about, things that happened to me that really stand out. They are all true — some I almost don't believe myself and I was there.

Looking back over the years, I was very lucky at times, more so than many other snake hunters out there. I found almost everything I was searching for and then some. While many of my friends and hunting companions are now retired or deceased, I'm still out there catching snakes. I'll never give that up. Hopefully, I'll die with a snake stick in my hand and a bag on my belt.

After my parents and I moved to Florida in the mid-1950s, I spent my whole life running around in the woods and swamps chasing one critter or another. I did the same thing in Connecticut for the first 18 years of my life, but there just weren't many snakes and no alligators up there. Deer, bird shooting, and fishing were good in New England, but there's nothing like the thrill of when I first starting catching snakes in Florida. I would be fishing along a canal somewhere when the next thing you'd know, I'd be chasing snakes. Fishing was forgotten about. Eventually, I completely substituted a snake stick and bag for the fishing rod unless I was trying to snag an alligator.

I used to go out every day or night depending on the time of year. In south Florida, you could hunt every day if you wanted. On the cooler days, you just had to dig a little in rotten stumps and other debris. On sunny cool days, snakes were lying around holes. On warmer days, they were crawling. At night, they were crawling, but you needed a light or you just road cruised – riding up and down the road looking for snakes.

Crazy things happened all the time and this is my story.

I hope you enjoy my adventures as much as I enjoyed doing them.

Frank Weed

My First Snakes

I have always enjoyed catching snakes even garter and ribbon snakes when I was six years old and living in Connecticut. I once purchased a Florida garter snake that I was quite fond of. She had about 20 babies late in the fall — too late to turn them loose. I made a terrarium for them, but I probably kept it too damp.

I kept them alive on salamanders, but fall was really cold, and the ground became frozen. I found a little spring behind the barn and it never became frozen. I could dig worms in the unfrozen ground next to the spring. The snake babies were five inches long and they really liked the worms. I cut them up in little pieces so the snakes could eat them.

Looking back, I realize I should have put calcium powder on the worms and the little pieces of fish that I was feeding to the babies. Calcium helps the snakes to digest the worms easier and I managed to keep most of the babies alive until spring when I could catch more salamanders, polliwogs and tiny frogs. The garter snakes were fun; they are alert and have a good personality.

They can also live for years with the right care. My friend Raymond Ditmar (world renowned herpetologist, writer, public speaker, and pioneering natural history filmmaker) had a pet garter snake for over twelve years.

When my family had the hunting preserve in Brookfield Center Connecticut, I turned every rock on the 300 acres and caught milk snakes, garter snakes, ribbon snakes, water snakes, black racers, and hognose snakes. I found a dead copperhead at our school bus stop when I was ten. That was the only poisonous snake I ever found near home, and an article was written in the local paper about me identifying it.

When I was 13, an older guy took my friend, David Matthews, and me to Schagticoke Mountain near Kent, Connecticut to look for timber rattlesnakes. It was May 3rd. It was warm, but there was still snow in the hollows. The guy found three timber snakes, and he pointed each one to us as they were hard to see. He also showed us where a group of college kids had just about turned the mountain upside down looking for snakes. There was a bounty on the snakes at the time and the college kids were trying to raise money for a dance. This guy said these kids had a pickup truck filled with dead rattlers. I hope the dance was a huge success, because it sure was deadly on the timber snakes.

When I was 14 and out bird hunting with a friend, we saw what we thought was a copperhead snake. My friend said to shoot it before it got away. I did shoot it before I realized it was just a water snake. I have been sorry about that shooting ever since. It was the first and last snake I ever killed.

A couple of years later we moved to Florida, the snake hunting capital of the world. I was in heaven.

Old Snake Lover?

I was never sure exactly where my love for snakes came from, but my older sister Joyce may have discovered the reason. She found the following article in a New Canaan Historical Society publication.

The Old Stone Fort
by Charles Morton, April 29, 1948

There are the remains of a stone fort near New Canaan Connecticut built by Steven Weed. A soldier in the Revolution War, he was born in 1753. He was captured and imprisoned in this infamous Sugar House in Brooklyn, NY. He was finally released, (exchanged) in poor health and allegedly mentally unbalanced from being tortured! He insisted that the British would raid his home area, so he built a stone fort and stood sentinel for 9 years, the war was over long before this. People used to come and watch him drill, and he told them stories about the war.

One day a large black snake moved into the fort, sunning itself on the rocks. Steven seemed to think that the snake was his relief and wouldn't let anyone bother it. One day the snake went to another part of the fort (probably got too hot or cold) and Steven got so mad because the snake "left his post" that he killed it! (I guess he was crazy.)

Maybe this is why I love snakes so much and why I'm a little crazy.

Frank showing off one of the many poisonous snakes he caught on a regular basis.

Hooked on Snakes

This will date me, but I actually met the world-renown herpetologist Raymond Ditmars at one of his Saturday Morning Encounters shows at the Bronx Zoo. Mr. Dltmars was a curator at the zoo and was famous for his work with mammals, insects and especially reptiles. I was only six or seven at the time, too young to appreciate this famous herpetologist and his contribution to the world of science and natural history.

Well, on that morning, he gave me a boa to hold and I was hooked! Sure, I had caught garter and ribbon snakes on my way to school in Brookfield Center, Connecticut but a boa was so much more fascinating. By the way, I used garter snakes to torment my little female classmates. Today, I'm sorry for those antics but that is simply what little boys did in those days.

A few years later, I met Brad Bradford at a Sportsman Show in New York City who sunk the hook a little deeper on my love for snakes. My family had an animal exhibit there and Brad was displaying snakes.

In the nine days of the show, I did not miss one of Brad's programs which was performed four or five times daily. To me, his talk was spectacular, and I was sure he was capable of walking on water. Years later, I used to sell him snakes in Miami.

I sold him the cottonmouths and water snakes used in the movie "Wind Across the Everglades." Burl Ives starred as an unruly poacher who meets his demise from the fangs of a water moccasin.

I continued to sell quite a few snakes to Brad until I discovered most of them were being pickled. I then sold to other dealers supplying the pet reptile trade. I wanted my snakes to be used as pets and not as pickled snakes.

In grade school, I did a book report on Ross Allen (founder of Ross Allen Reptile Institute at Silver Springs, Florida) and a few years later I was selling him snakes. My sister Joyce worked for Ross at his business in Miami. My father and Ross almost established a crocodile farm in Jamaica but the government there was too uncooperative.

Many of my freshly caught snakes ended up with Bill Haast at the Miami Serpentarium in Miami, Florida. During these many exchanges, I often witnessed his feats with cobras, and it made me nervous every time.

Besides selling snakes to Bill Chase, I also worked taking care of the many snakes and other animals he imported. For once, I had some steady income, but my real life was being in the field catching snakes, not cleaning cages. So, this job was never going to last long.

I sold to and hunted snakes with Roy Van Nostrand. He now has one of the biggest reptile dealerships in the country, Strictly Reptiles.

Working with the top names in the reptile world as they were becoming famous, it increased my love for snakes and reptiles even more.

Turtles

Now I don't dislike turtles, but they just don't move me the way snakes do. I've kept turtles off and on all my life, mostly box turtles and gopher tortoises but also painted, softshell, snapper and cooter turtles.

The first turtle I can remember catching, I was about five, was a cute little thing with an orange spot on its head (this was in Connecticut). Many years later I found out it was a bog turtle. They are very rare and protected now. Over 65 years ago, there wasn't anything as protected species.

I can remember when I was about ten walking on our frozen pond and seeing a painted turtle walking very slowly on the bottom. I got a few feet ahead of the turtle, chopped a hole in the ice and grabbed the turtle when it got to my hole. I had to put it in my shirt to keep it from freezing!

My sister Joyce and I were walking around behind a friend's house one day. There was a river back there called the Still River. It was a tributary of the Housatonic River. This wasn't a very big river, maybe 40 feet wide. It also flowed north where we were, which was unusual, and it was very polluted. It flowed through Danbury, Connecticut, the capital of the state. One day the river would be green, the next day brown, the next day blue as the factories dumped their used dye in the river. It has since been cleaned up.

Anyway, back to the turtles. The river was also used by some mills and the water would go up and down at different times. That day the water was down, and there were some mud flats here and there. I could see some lumps in the mud, and I waded out to see what they were. Poking in the mud, I found a snapping turtle. I happened to have a bag with me so I dropped it in. The turtle was about five pounds. It was a big one!

Joyce and I caught a couple more about the same size, but then I saw a large lump and thought there was more than one there. I poke around and out came the biggest turtle I had ever seen. This one had to be 25 or 30 pounds or more. I dragged it up to the bank and tried to get it in the bag. I dumped the little ones out, but this monster was too wide. I tried to carry it by the tail, but it kept trying to bite me, and I couldn't hold it far enough away from my leg.

I finally had an idea and I turned it over on its back and put sticks all around it to pin it down and pen it up. Then we ran back to the house to get my father's help. By the time we got back, the turtle had rolled over and escaped, but it was a thrill to see one that big, especially when you are about ten years old!

I used to catch a box turtle now and then in Connecticut, but they were never that common. There were places in Texas and Florida where I could find 30 or 40 a day. I was in the middle of Texas one time just driving around when I came to an area that was pretty open pasture with little clumps of bushes. It was pretty hot, but the bushes looked like they would be cool enough for some snakes to hide under, so I parked and walked out to look around.

Pulling the bushes aside with my snake hook (only a fool uses his hands), I started to find box turtles, one, two, sometimes four or five together. I was able to fill a few bags with all I could carry.

In Florida, we lived not too far from the Everglades but nearer the dryer side. One day, after a fire and it had cooled down, I went out to see what I could find. Fires were always good to hunt after. All the cover is burned off and you can see more easily. I walked along poking in the rabbit and armadillo holes with my snake hook hoping to find a rattlesnake or something. I did find a rattler, but I also found over twenty box turtles. Even though the holes were only two or three feet deep, they were perfectly shaped. The fires burn so fast and quick it doesn't burn up all the oxygen and the holes provided an escape from being cooked. I did find a few dead turtles that were too far from a hole and a dead rat snake that was up a tree that the fire totally consumed but that was all. With all the fires that I have hunted after, I have found very few dead reptiles.

I used to catch a lot of softshell turtles. They are pretty neat looking, and the babies are cute — the Seminole Indians are now raising them for food. I tried to catch a very large softshell one day as it was crossing the Tamiami Trail heading for the canal. I parked and jumped out.

They are very fast when they want to be, but I got it by its hind legs just as it was heading into the canal. The bank was pretty steep and I couldn't get any traction. I was lying on pine needles and both of my hands were busy with the turtle's legs. Consequently, the turtle proceeded to drag me into the canal until I had to let it go. That was the biggest turtle I ever lost. Oh, well, you can't catch them all.

Lion

This happened over 50 years ago, but I remember it well. My father used to rent animals of all kinds to just about anyone and for whatever purpose — movies, TV, fairs, anything. I remember one time being dragged down the main street of Bridgeport, Connecticut by a 150- pound bear on a rope. I guessed the bear didn't like what the band behind me was playing.

A movie theater in Newark, New Jersey wanted to rent an African lion for a weekend to promote a "Tarzan" movie. Dad said he could supply one but, in fact, we didn't own one at that time. We did know a friend who had two lions. One lion was pretty tame, but the other wasn't.

"We'll take the tame one," Dad said. The day came when we were supposed to pick up the lion. We pulled into the guy's yard and he said he had been trying to get in touch with us. The tame lion had died that morning, but we were welcome to use the untamed one. Since we really didn't have a choice, we loaded Mr. Untame into a crate and headed for New Jersey.

At the theater, we set up a cage in the lobby with a few potted palms around it and settled in for the weekend. I had a six-foot boa snake to add a little extra to the display. Well, the customers began to come for the afternoon matinee. They would come over and look into the cage and the lion would roar and jump at the bars. We finally moved the barricade to keep the people further away, but the lion still raised ruckus. The theater manager said not to worry, it was great publicity!

A little later, there were sirens wailing and all kinds of excitement out in the street. Then a bunch of cops came in and said we had to remove the lion immediately. It seems someone almost had a stroke every time the lion roared. The police talked to the manager briefly and then he said to load up the lion. The manager was very pleased because of all the publicity he was receiving.

The management evacuated the theater and the state police blocked off the street (lights were flashing everywhere) so the lion could be moved. Troopers covered the lobby with Thompson Sub Machine Guns. There I was, an eleven-year-old kid thinking I was in an "Untouchables" movie with Elliot Ness.

The lion loaded with no trouble. No one got shot, but some of those gun-wielding cops made me nervous. I wasn't sure what they might do. The manager paid us the full price. He said he couldn't put a price on that much publicity. A state trooper escorted us to the New York state line. My only regret was I didn't get to see the end of the movie.

Snakes in the Walls

We moved several times after we got to Florida. One of the houses we lived in was near Davie, close to Ft. Lauderdale. It was out in the country and surrounded by fields.

I was putting some things in the attic crawl space one day when I saw some shedded snakeskins. "This could be good," I thought to myself. "I will not have to even leave the house to catch snakes!" I crawled around the attic space several different times on different days and never found a thing. Oh, well, it looked good.

One night, Dad was in bed reading and called me. I went into the bedroom and he said, "I can hear a snake crawling inside the wall."

I didn't hear anything but I'm deaf as a post, too much shooting and riding around in an airboat all day. We didn't know about mufflers or ear plugs back then. I put my ear up to the wall and I could hear a scraping sound. I waited until the sound got near the ceiling and then I climbed up into the crawl space and there was a nice four-foot red rat snake. There was only a one-inch space between the cement block wall and the drywall, but it was big enough for the snake to crawl through.

We only lived there about a year and during that time I caught about 25 red and yellow rat snakes; plus, one scarlet king snake. I was happy about catching all those snakes and I didn't even have to leave the house.

Pet Python

While working at one of the animal importers, it must have been Chase's, I used to see this attractive woman now and then. One of my coworkers said she was married so I didn't look much.

One day she came over and introduced herself as Jackie. She said she had a pet python and I should come by and see it sometime.

"Sure," I said. Girls and snakes together, what more could I ask for? A week later I was in her neighborhood, so I looked her up.

She lived in a trailer park in a medium size trailer. I found her number and parked. She invited me in to meet Lefty. She told me to sit on the couch and she'd bring him in. She went in the back, I heard a door open, she came back and sat down beside me.

I started to ask her where the snake was when I heard a rustling sound and then this HUGE head comes up on the couch followed by a massive neck and body. It crawled across our laps, around the back of the trailer, back up the hallway, and the tail was still coming down the hallway.

It was the biggest snake I had ever seen. Just as calm as could be, she said Lefty was 24 or 25 feet, she had not been able to measure him lately.

I helped, with five other guys, to measure a 28-foot reticulated python one time and almost couldn't do it. Reticulated pythons are considered to be the longest in the world. Lefty was just as big or bigger than the reticulated python I had once measured.

She told me her favorite story. A guy she had just met came by one day. He knew her husband was a tall skinny guy and he knew they were separated. He asked if her husband ever came by. He didn't want her husband to show up in case he got "lucky."

Jackie said, "You don't have worry about him, the snake ate him!" The guy got up and left and never came back. She was my kind of girl! Too bad I wasn't into girls at the time. I was too busy snake hunting. We could have had fun!

Goldfish

My parents and I were doing a Sportsman Show one January in Hartford, Connecticut or Burlington, Vermont. I'm not which because we did so many that they just kind of ran together.

I was about 14 at the time. We had a snake and animal exhibit there. I used to go to the shows as often as school allowed. I had a garter snake that I used to take everywhere.

It was cold there in January, so I carried it inside my shirt. The snake was hungry, and I didn't have any of my frozen frogs with me that it usually ate. I found a 5 and 10-cent store not far from the show building. A buddy and I walked in and found the fish department. I had the snake in my shirt. They had a large aquarium full of goldfish. They were only 10 or 15 cents apiece.

A salesgirl came by to help us. I said, "I would like four goldfish please."

She got a net and a little paper container. She dipped one out and said, "This is a pretty one." I said I didn't care what they looked like since they were going to be snake food. She looked like she didn't believe me, so I took the fish out of the net and held it in front of my shirt.

The snake came out, grabbed the fish and went back inside my shirt to eat it. The salesgirl left. I can't imagine what got into her!

Finally, a salesman came by and got me three more goldfish. I paid for them and took them back to the show where the guests would appreciate the feedings.

The Cross-Eyed Rattler

Working the Sportsman Shows with my parents was always fun! We were always doing something different — animals at one show, snakes at another, shooting or fishing demonstrations at another or all of the above.

I can't remember where we were because it was 50 or so years ago but I was putting on a rattlesnake handling show. This type of show was called a "thrill" show and Dad was the Master of Ceremonies.

Typically, I would arrive with a box containing four or five large diamondbacks, dump them onto the floor, and play around with them.

They would repeatedly strike at me at first but, after a week or so, they became tame or died from too much handling. Therefore, we often needed new snakes. It wouldn't be a very exciting show if the rattlers didn't strike at me.

I wore motorcycle boots that came almost to my knees. They didn't have snake proof boots in those days or, maybe, I didn't know about them. The boots I did use, however, were never punctured.

Anyway, I was on stage letting them strike at me and most of the snakes were missing. I had a balloon that I stuck onto my snake stick. Sometimes, one would strike at it and break it but, most of the time, I would hold it next to my boot.

The rattlers felt the heat from my body and while striking at me they would break the balloon. This particular time, however, the snake struck not at my ankle where I thought it was clearly looking but right at my kneecap above the boot.

I just froze waiting for the pain I thought was coming. Dad was right there and asked, "Did it get you?" I felt absolutely nothing. It was dramatic, however, and the entire building was totally silent. Dad and I realized the rattler had struck without opening its mouth. I was lucky. This was even better than a "dry bite" which is where you are bitten but no venom is injected.

I always knew I was lucky, but that day was really my lucky day. I pinned all the rattlers, put them in the box and went back to the dressing room to get ready for the next performance. For the next few shows, I was wary of the cross-eyed rattler.

Gator in the Pool

Once again, my parents and I were working a Sportsman Show. Most of these shows had a large pool of water about 20 by 40 feet and then 4 feet deep. There were lumberjacks who competed in log-rolling, canoe tilting, and various other water exhibitions. Most of these guys were quite good.

At one of these shows, we had an Alligator Hunt. We had to come up with new ideas every year when we went back to those shows. People expected something new and different every year. This was in January or February and there was snow on the ground.

To fill the pool, a fire hose was run from an outside hydrant into the pool. This water was really cold. It required two days for the pool to warm up. Our act was to put one of our eight-foot gators in the pool, dim the house lights, get into a canoe, shine a spotlight around, paddle around, and put a noose around the gator's neck. Then we would pull it out of the pool and onto the stage and tie it up.

Sounds simple, right? Well, the water was so cold that the gator sank to the bottom and stayed there. The water was so murky that we couldn't see the gator. Dad jumped in and waded around but couldn't find it. We left it there.

Now the show must go on and our act was followed by the log-rolling and canoe tilting. The lumberjacks really put on a show that night. The ones that got knocked off the logs or thrown out of the canoes barely hit the water before they leaped out of the pool. The thought of sharing the pool with a gator kept even the losers dry, or reasonably so.

After the last act, Dad and I got in the pool and finally found the gator. After putting a noose on it, we pulled it out. We loaded it into a crate and shut the door. I looked around and to my amazement, everyone was still in the stands, two thousand people or more. One guy asked later if we did that every show. The answer was no.

Crocodiles don't grow small in Florida

Miss Vermont

My parents and I were working at a Sportsman Show in Hartford, Connecticut. I had a bunch of snakes on exhibition and I played with a few rattlesnakes on the stage a couple of times a day. I was about seventeen at the time.

There were a lot of sports celebrities walking around promoting different products, signing autographs, etc. I once met Jim Thorpe, the Indian athlete who starred in the 1936 Olympic games at one of the shows just after I had done a book report on him. I don't think I washed my hand for a week. I was impressed!

However, the one that made the biggest impression was a girl, Charlene King Johnson, who was Miss Vermont in one of the Miss America contests. She used to walk around, sort of as a good-will ambassador. She sure was cuter than all the jocks.

She would come by our exhibit and talk now and then since she liked snakes. I loved her being around her. Sometimes, when she was getting too much attention from some of the guys, she would "borrow" my indigo snake and carry it around her neck. It worked most of the time as even males do not like snakes. She had fun with it and named it Inky. Every indigo snake I have had since then has been called called Inky

About six months later, we were doing another show in White River Junction, Vermont. We were exhibiting in a tent and the show ran for six days. I met a girl there named Mary Sanville. Her father had a pony ride ring there, and we hit it off pretty good and spent a lot of time together. I was just beginning to really notice girls. I had always been too busy hunting, fishing, and chasing snakes to chase girls.

One afternoon Mary and I were in the tent cleaning cages occupied by snakes, monkeys, lizards, baby bears, etc. It was the quiet time of the day when we could get a lot of work done without too many people around.

Anyway, all of a sudden, this beautiful girl comes up and throws her arms around me and gives me a big hug. It was Charlene Johnson, Miss Vermont.

"Frank, so good to see you again, do you still have Inky?" I did. About then, I turned around to introduce Charlene to Mary and Mary was gone. Apparently, she was the jealous type!

I finally found Mary and got everything straightened out. She even liked Charlene, although they used to fight, friendly, over who was going to carry Inky around. It was a good thing that I had a friendly boa constrictor for whoever wasn't handling Inky.

South American Rodeo

Dad and I took a job working and running a rodeo in Venezuela, South America. I ended up down there for three months. We rounded up a bunch of cowboys and four or five horses to take down. I was to do a trick shooting act like Annie Oakley. The promoter down there was Jose "Latigo" Zalaya, who also did a whip act. We loaded all our gear on a four-engine Constellation plane along with the horses. Before taking off, the pilot came out and asked, "Who is the best shot in the group?"

Everyone said I was. So, he said, "Here's a loaded gun. If any of the horses get loose and start ramming around, shoot them so they don't wreck the plane." He added, "Try not to put too many holes in the plane!"

The flight was uneventful, thank goodness, and I got to talk with the stewardess since I was awake the whole time.

We landed in Maricaibo with no trouble. The plane's door was ten or twelve feet above the ground. A guy came out with a forklift with a pallet on it and wanted the horses to stand on it while he lowered it to the ground. This would not work!

The horses would have jumped off and broken their necks or be severely injured. We finally found some more pallets, made a chute, blindfolded the horses, and all went well.

The rodeo was fun, and I got to travel around a lot. I mostly only worked on weekends, but I did do some promotions at schools during the week. I was disappointed that I did not see more snakes. I only caught a few, a blunt-headed tree snake and a tropical rat snake up under a bullring.

I always liked to look at the local people, especially the girls. I hoped to see someone I knew, although there was a small chance of that. However, once, as we were waiting at the airport for our flight home, I happened to look over at a girl across the lobby and there was the stewardess from the plane on our trip down. She was talking to a guy, but I could not see his face. I went over to say hello, and the person she was talking with was a guy I used to sell snakes to in Florida. It was Ralph Curtis from Wild Cargo. What a small world! I think he was heading to Brazil.

Catching snakes in other countries is fun!

Ross Heilman - Stage Name, Kananga

Of all the people I know, with the exception of my father, I think Ross Kananga was the most fearless. He'd tackle almost anything. We first worked together at a western tourist attraction, Pioneer City, near Ft. Lauderdale, Florida. He played an Indian half-breed gunfighter doing gun fights and stunt work. His nickname was Red Hand. After work some days, we'd go catch a few snakes.

Then we worked together in a rodeo in Venezuela, South America for three months. We put on gunfights and bank robberies between the rodeo events. Ross also rode the bucking horses and Brahma bulls. They wouldn't let me ride anything because I was doing a trick shooting show and they didn't want me breaking anything that would impair my shooting ability. I got to be the Sheriff and Ross was one of the bad guys. In every show I got to shoot him, with blanks of course.

One day we went out looking for snakes. We never had much free time, and the only woods we could find were about third growth and not very big. I finally found a tree that was big enough to have a rotten spot in it. I poked around a little and out came a blunt-headed tree snake. It was about three feet long and as big around as a pencil with a big head. They are rear-fanged but not dangerous. I caught a gecko later, which the snake promptly bit, paralyzing it instantly and then he ate it. The only other snake I caught down there was a tropical rat snake that showed up in the bullring stalls.

Later Ross started an alligator farm in Florida. He had it for a while but sold it and moved to Jamaica where he started a crocodile farm. He personally caught over 200 crocs in the wild. They used to be very common. I saw over a hundred in less than a week of hunting.

Ross was a double for James Bond in the movie "Live and Let Die". Parts of the movie were filmed at his place. The bad guys had taken Bond to an island to be eaten by crocodiles. Ross as Bond was supposed to jump to shore across the backs of three crocs. He didn't make it the first try. He has the pictures and scars from where the ten-foot croc was chewing on his legs. I also have a souvenir tooth from that croc that is as big as my thumb.

Ross' house was the heroin factory in the movie that was set on fire by Bond. The film crew put it out and I stayed there for a week. Ross's stage name "Kananga" was used for the bad guy in the film. I heard he got $50,000 for the stunt work. That kind of money can make you pretty brave!

Illustrate what kind of guy of Ross was he came by one day and asked me to show him some tricks on wrestling gators. It seems someone offered him a job wrestling alligators and he took the job without knowing much about it. How's that for confidence?

A year later I saw him beat the best Indian alligator wrestler at a tribal fair with more daring feats. He even beat James Billie (now Chief), and that took some doing!

The last time I was in Jamaica with Ross, I had two premonitions. I felt he was getting a little careless with some of his crocs and also with an African lion he had raised from a cub but was now a 250-pound lump of claws He said he'd be careful but he wasn't,

Ross always carried a .357 mag hand gun whenever he went into the cat enclosure. The cage was a half-acre surrounded by a ten-foot tall fence. He went in one day and got between the male and the female. The male didn't like that. The lion approached and grabbed Ross by the left forearm and bit down hard. Ross had enough presence of mind to shoot it twice in the head.

The lion let him go and walked away. It lived for another two years with the bullets still in its head. Ross just wanted to let it go. A month later, one of the crocs bit him in the same spot.

A year or two later, Ross moved back to Florida. Unrest in Jamaica scared all the tourists away. He brought back a bunch of crocs, two African lions, and two black leopards with him.

He was keeping them at a tourist attraction in Ft. Lauderdale. I was there one day and Ross was in a cage playing with his black leopards. The male was over 100 pounds and I could see that male cat looking for an opportunity to get him. This was another premonition I had.

Just a few days later, he turned his back on the cat as he went out the door. I always back out, look them in the eye as do all the people who play with the big cats. Anyway, the cat jumped on his back and knocked him down, held onto his shoulders with his front claws while raking his back and legs with his back claws. Lastly, he bit him in the head.

Luckily, Ross had the foresight to have a rifle behind the fence and the tour guides knew where it was and what it was for. Equally lucky, a tour guide came by right at that time. The guide, a girl only 17 and on the job for only a few weeks, jumped the fence, grabbed the rifle and shot the leopard off his back. At the same time, the female leopard came out and grabbed Ross's dog and killed it with a bite to its head. The girl shot and killed it too. She earned her pay that day. One of the tourists jokingly asked, "Do they do this at every show?"

Ross was in the hospital almost a week and he was never the same after that. Ross moved out to the Everglades. A short while later, he was out in a canoe with his aunt and he dropped dead from a heart attack. He fell from the canoe; he was only 35 years old. I was living nearby when some people brought his aunt to my house.

I went back to look for Ross. I really didn't want to find him dead, and I didn't. All I found was his hat. The police divers found him a few hours later right where I was looking. I think he knew I didn't want to find him and waited for the divers. The divers had known Ross because he had taught them karate and they identified him by all his scars.

I heard that he had an infection in his brain from the leopard bite, which probably helped bring on his heart attack. I still miss him. There was never a dull moment when he was around!

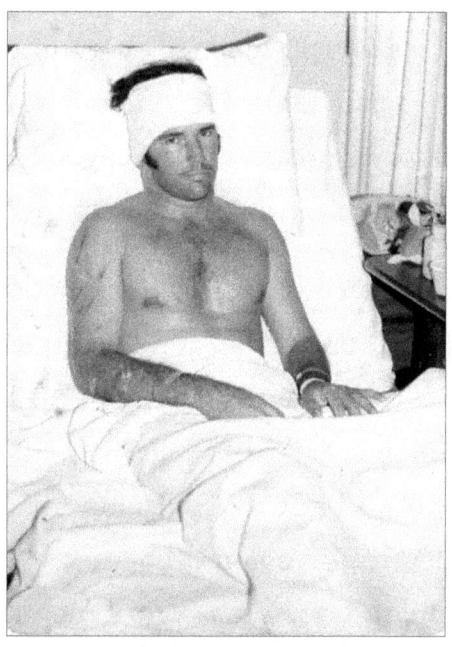

Ross Heilman aka Kananga

Arthur Jones

Once upon a time, I worked with Arthur Jones of the Nautilus body building machines and other ventures. He had a TV show similar to Marlin Perkins' Zoo Parade called Wild Capture. Its emphasis was on catching animals rather than how they lived.

Arthur wanted to do adventure shows all over the country with alligator wrestling, poisonous snake handling and showing various wild animals. He wanted me to do some shooting demonstrations indoors with the bullet backstop suspended from the ceiling. I was to also help with the snakes and my father was to help manage everything. The first show was to be in Cincinnati, Ohio. He rented part of the Music Hall and set up display areas, snake cages, and an alligator wrestling pool. He advertised in all the papers and on TV.

Arthur decided he needed more alligators than we had, so he ordered some from Miami. Dad and I went down to the airport at Opa Locka, Florida to help load them. We loaded them into an old B-25 bomber that Arthur had. Something came up and the plane had to go back to Louisiana for a few days. We, however, decided to drive and drove north to Cincinnati. We arrived there only a few hours before the plane was to land. Dad went to the airport with some of Arthur's workers to get the gators. I was needed elsewhere and would miss all the action. There was a TV crew and news-paper reporters who were doing stories on the 25 alligators coming to town.

Well, the pilot radioed that he couldn't get his wheels down and was unsure of what to do. Airport officials decided to put foam down on the runway and have him try a belly landing. First, he needed to circle to bum up most of the fuel before making what could be a hairy landing. The plane circled for an hour giving time for another film crew to set up.

Arthur's alligator wrestler was on the plane and opted not to come down with the plane. He had sky-dived a few times, and there was a parachute on board. With cameras recording, he opened the door and jumped out over the field. However, he didn't duck enough and hit his head on the tail of the plane knocking him unconscious. Now he was tumbling through the air.

Thankfully, the cold air revived him and he got the chute opened just in time. The plane made a perfect belly landing and the fire trucks along the runway weren't necessary. I later found out that this pilot had been in a fiery crash one time. So, as the plane was skidding to a stop the pilot popped the windshield and jumped out.

All of this was recorded on film. It was shown all over the country and my father had his picture on the front page of hundreds of newspapers with a six-foot alligator draped over his shoulder. We almost got more publicity than we wanted. I could only see it on TV.

Arthur himself was a bit of a daredevil. He had a thing he did with rattlers that even I wouldn't do. It was the ultimate free handling of diamondbacks. He would take a wild diamondback, dump it on the ground, and get close enough to grab it. Then with a lightning-fast move, he would slam his hand down on the snake's head, press it to the ground, and pick it up by the neck. I saw him do this many times and he was never bitten.

It was very hard on the snakes and many of them died shortly after this treatment. I know it can be done because I saw him do it, but you had better be fast and not miss! It was a great stunt, but the odds were against you--it only takes one miss and you are in a lot of trouble. I never considered trying it. To say the least, Arthur was an exciting guy to be around.

Gator Needed in Oklahoma

My friend, Chief James Billie of the Seminole Tribe, called one day and asked if I wanted to take a little trip. I figured why not as snake hunting was slow and I needed a change. He needed someone to take an alligator to Stillwater, Oklahoma. The last guy he had hired put the eight-foot alligator in the back of a camper on a pickup. He got about 400 miles away and stopped at a rest area. This guy went to the back of the truck, and the door was open. The gator was gone. He backtracked but didn't find the gator. James was a little upset to say the least.

The Chief said the gator had to be in Oklahoma in three days, so I would have to leave right away on the 1700-mile trip. He wanted me to drive his new pickup, so we went over to the reservation and caught an eight-foot gator. We put some hay in the truck bed and a section of fencing tied down on top. This arrangement made a good cage for the gator. James gave me some cash, a gas card, and away I went.

I stopped to fuel up nearby which was a good thing. I discovered the truck had a locking gas cap and he hadn't given me the key. I had to go back and hunt James up for the key and away I went again.

The trip was uneventful. I just stopped for gas and food and to pour some water on the gator now and then. A couple of short sleeps in motels and I was there in the middle of the afternoon before the deadline date. James had flown out and met me at the Indian-owned Bingo Hall. We put the gator in a canvas pool in a closet and added water and locked the door.

James and I went to town for some food and other items he said he needed. We got a burger and then went to a clothing store. The Chief started trying on shirts. James had a man's purse — kind of half a saddlebag that he had to lay down when he tried on clothing. He told me to keep my eyes on the bag as he often left it behind.

Wouldn't you know it, he went to another area and left the purse. I retrieved it and caught up to him and said, "Here, you forgot this again."

"Oh, good," he said. "I'd hate to lose it, I've got $10,000 in cash in there." He got me a room at the Holiday Inn and then he took off for somewhere else.

For some reason, I still wasn't tired of driving, so I went out and drove a few dirt roads. I found some nice speckled king snakes and a few other snakes and suddenly jet lag kicked in. Back at the hotel, I crashed.

James had told me that the show wasn't until 1 pm, so I slept in. I got up, had breakfast, and road hunted for a little while. Yes, I was looking for snakes.

However, it was cool and nothing was crawling. Back at the Bingo Hall, I parked out of the way since the place was full of busses that had arrived full of bingo players. As I exited the truck, I saw a piece of tin in the field. I cannot resist tin. So, I picked it up and found a nice six-foot bull snake hiding underneath it. My day was made!

I went in to watch the bingo players — all 5,000 of them. One guy won $50,000 on one game, and he was paid in cash. The operators had two guys with guns escort him to his car. If he was smart, he should have hired them to escort him to a bank. The Bingo Hall finally took a lunch break so players and workers could eat. Later, there was an entertainment break, and that's when James did his gator wrestling stint.

We had a small pool set up in the establishment. Periodically, James would jump in with the gator, get it moving, and splashing everyone. He worked for less than ten minutes. I didn't have to do anything but be there in case something went wrong.

After the show, James said, "Load it up and take it home."

He gave me an ungodly amount of money and said he'd see me next week. It was always fun doing business with James! I loaded up the gator, snakes, and went back to Florida. Another 1,700 miles of travel but I did it slower this time.

Ross Heilman aka Kananga and crocodile at a wild animal show

Snake Lecture

There was this guy in Fort Lauderdale that used to come by now and then and bring me snakes. He occasionally gave snake lectures to various groups. He was not real knowledgeable, but he was an interesting speaker and he liked snakes.

One day he came by with a guy who had a pet boa constrictor that he wanted to show me. I think my friend was thinking about buying it and wanted me to check it out. I gave my approval. They looked at all my snakes and we talked for a while. As they were leaving, my friend said something I guess I did not hear quite right about a Grand Dragon. I thought he was talking about lizards.

A few weeks later, the guy who was selling the boa constrictor called and said he had a problem — it seems my friend was supposed to give a snake lecture at a youth meeting, but he had to go out of town. He wondered if I could take his place? He would pay twenty-five dollars. I thought why not?

He gave me directions to a warehouse in Fort Lauderdale. So I put a bunch of snakes, turtles, a small gator and a crocodile in some bags and off I went. I do not like to talk much but get me started on snakes and I do pretty well. I had enough critters to keep a few kids happy for a while.

It was only about ten miles to the place, but the directions were not very good. I finally found the place and four guys came out to help me carry the bags in. We went through the door and started down a hall.

One guy was in front and the others were behind me. After turning down another hallway, hanging on the wall were all these white robes with peaked hoods and a neon cross!

Suddenly my friend's words hit me, "Grand Dragon". I was in the headquarters of the Klu Klux Klan for south Florida. I thought about backing out, but there were more of them in back of me than in front, so I sucked it up and did the talk. I have no idea what I said because I was so nervous.

There were about fifty people there, mostly kids and I guess everything was okay, but I was sure glad to get out of there.

Learning the Tricks of the Trade

The hardest thing about snake hunting in a new area is finding where the snakes are and the best time to catch them. Some places you have to hunt in the daytime, others at night and sometimes mornings or evenings. Once you have found them and when they are out, the rest is easy.

When my father and I first went snake hunting, we would drive somewhere, park the car, and walk out in to the woods, fields, or swamps. We found ourselves combating mosquitoes, briers, water, mud, and the sun. It gets very hot in Florida and we did not find many snakes! We were finding enough to keep us fairly happy, but we were working pretty hard at it.

Heading back to Miami from one of these outings, we saw two young guys hitchhiking along Route 27 south of Clewiston. They each had three bags full of snakes. No one was giving them a ride because of the snakes. We pulled over and asked if they wanted a ride. Yes, they did. We asked them where they had caught all the snakes and they said right here, along the right of way on the shoulder.

We had a hard time believing this, so they said pull over and we will show you. We pulled over and parked. They got out and walked with us along the road. In a few minutes we had found a nice king snake. Simple and after all that hard work we used to go through.

These kids would hitch a ride out to the Everglades, walk along the road catching snakes until they could not carry anymore, and then hitch a ride back. They said they were saving up to buy a car. I bet they got one too.

What I do know is we never walked or waded out in the swamp again unless we wanted to. It was so much easier walking along the road catching the snakes.

Fort Matanzas Rattlers

After we moved to Florida in 1955, one of the first people I met was a guy everyone just called Woody. I don't remember his last name, maybe I never knew it. He was just Woody. He was a lot like me, so that is why we got along. He spent most of his time in the woods looking for whatever snakes, turtles, and things to eat. He was mostly into turtles and even started a turtle farm. However, it never amounted to much.

One day he said he was going to take me out diamondback rattlesnake hunting on an island he knew about. I said, "I'm ready."

I had never caught a diamondback rattlesnake before. We loaded up our little pram in the station wagon and went about ten miles up the road. We parked and put the pram in the inlet that con-nected to the intercoastal waterway below St. Augustine. Woody said the island was named Rattlesnake Island.

There was an old Spanish fort at one end that made it interesting too. It was Fort Matanzas. It wasn't very big, but it didn't need to be since there was no way a boat could get by. Only about a hundred yards wide, a few cannons could control the area. We paddled over and beached the boat near clumps of brush and small trees. The sand was white and beautiful.

Woody said the rattlers lived in the gopher tortoise holes, which can be ten feet and 40 feet long. He said there was usually a pile of sand near the hole which made them easy to see. We walked around in the brush for a while and saw a tortoise hole.

I walked over and tried to look down the hole but couldn't see anything. Then Woody came over and said that when rattlers exited the holes to warm up they usually lay about six feet from the holes. He also said that there was a rattler about four feet behind me lying in the grass that I never saw. I quickly moved a little farther away. Then we caught it. Now I always look around any tortoise hole before I go up to it.

We found and caught two more rattlers as we made our way along. The sun was pretty strong for someone just down from Connecticut, so I'd stand in the shade of some small trees for a few minutes periodically. In one clump of wax myrtle I found a nice corn snake and then another a few clumps away. It was the only cool spot on the island for the snakes or, for that matter, me. The rattlers could stay down a nice cool tortoise burrow. Those clumps were only about twenty feet thick, but it was pretty bare in the middle. I could just stick my head inside and be able to see if there was anything there. I still find snakes in places like that.

Now I think there is a road down the middle of the island but I doubt if there are any rattlers left. I'm grateful that Woody took pity on a poor Yankee kid who didn't know where to look for snakes, but I learned fast.

A Smart Rattler

When we first moved to Florida in the 1950's, my family rented a house way out in the sticks, which is how I liked it. The house was a few miles north of Flagler Beach. Today it is Palm Coast, but back then it was pretty wild. I did not have a car for awhile and it was hard learning the country. A friend took pity on me and gave me an old pickup truck. It was a 1941 Chevy, kind of rusty but it ran good and it was mine!

A local guy said I ought to make it into a beach buggy. A skeeter they called them. Once I decided to do that, we took the doors, hood and the bed off. We put on some old big tires we found lying around and just made a wooden platform for the back. I bolted a big wooden box with a lid on the back to put snakes and things in and away we went.

It was similar to a jeep, which was good because the beach sand was very soft here, not like down at Daytona Beach where it was hard as a rock. There were lots of little sand roads around that we would ride looking for snakes or whatever. The highway that went by the house was A1A and it paralleled the ocean most of the way.

However, where we were, it went inland for about five miles putting the ocean more or less a half- mile away. There were some very thick palmettos just west of the ocean. They were so thick you could not walk very far but I got to riding up and down the little sand roads. I started catching a few diamondbacks all except on this one road. I would drive up this one road, looking for places where a snake had crossed the sand. Evidence of their crossing was easy to see.

Many times, I would drive up to the ocean, turn around, drive back and there would be a snake track over my tire tracks. It was a big snake too, had to be over six feet by the width of the track. I kept going up this road at different times of the day hoping to find the snake in the road, you could not see five feet in the palmettos, but I never caught it. I would even go halfway up the road, sit there in the middle of the road for a half hour at a time and never see it. A couple of times I found its track over the top of my tracks, like it knew when I wasn't looking for a second.

I am sure I would have caught it eventually, but we moved down to south Florida. After the move, I never got back up that way much. The area is a wildlife preserve now and hopefully that snake has passed its smarts along to the next generation. That was the smartest snake I never caught.

Bugs, Spiders and Snakes for Sale

When my parents and I first moved down to the Miami area, it took me some time to get to know where to hunt. Once I learned the lay of the land, I started finding all sorts of critters. It was a lot wilder back in the 1950's, but there weren't many places to sell the critters I was catching. I had taken 52 cottonmouth moccasins up to Ross Allen's Reptile Institute in Silver Springs to sell since no one in Miami wanted them. Ross took them without hesitating. I met a guy there that worked for and with Ross. I believe his name was Bill Smith. He went around and bought animals from people and brought them back to Ross.

Bill would buy just about anything — bugs, turtles, snakes, and spiders. He and Ross would then sell them to schools and colleges for biology labs. Many of these animals he would buy already pickled.

Bill would come by every week or two and buy whatever you had. He even left me boxes of jars, vials, and preservatives. At different times, different critters would come out. They would be out for a few days and then they would be gone.

One time, I went to a shopping center, and there were large floodlights in the parking lot. Under those lights were thousands of water boatman beetles. I just scooped them up with a shovel and filled 21-gallon jars and added some alcohol.

I got one dollar a gallon for them, which was good in those days of 25 cent gasoline. I used to catch a lot of scorpions, the big black ones, but I never killed them. I even had one for a pet. This was before people kept scorpions and arachnids as pets and I was fond of them!

I collected all kinds of spiders and I never killed them either. I think I only got 5, 10, or 25 cents for them. Garter and ribbon snakes were worth only 10 cents each. I just recently collected a large black widow spider and got eight dollars for it. So much for the good old days.

After a while, more and more places started buying snakes and the competition started boosting the prices we were paid. Sometimes we snake hunters would call several places to see which one was paying the most.

One dealer might be paying 10 cents more a foot than the other guy and he would get all the snakes. Then the next dealer would beat that price and he would get all the snakes. This rivalry was great for us snake hunters.

Scarlet king snakes started at $1, $3, and $5 for small, medium or large snakes. A week later another dealer might be paying $3, $5, and $7. Today dealers pay over fifty dollars for a large scarlet king snake.

I caught twelve one night thirty years ago and, at today's prices, I would be wealthy. I can still make as much, if not more nowadays, just by finding a few snakes because of the price difference. How-ever, catching more snakes made it more exciting. I know past hunters didn't catch all the snakes, but the environment has changed. There are still a few places that are loaded with snakes but not many. Less frogs mean less snakes that eat frogs. Less swamps mean less swamp-loving critters. Unfortunately, it will probably get worse before it gets better.

Snake Bites

When my parents and I first moved to Miami, Florida, we didn't know anyone in the snake business. After asking around, we got a few names of guys that caught snakes. We looked up the first guy on the list, he agreed to take us out on his airboat and maybe find some snakes. His name was Harry Peterson, an old snake hunter, who caught snakes mostly for their skins. He related how he used to go out and fill a 50-gallon barrel in a few days. We said we wanted the snakes alive. Harry said that was okay as there wasn't a market for skins anymore. He was mostly catching frogs now for their legs.

The water was very high that year which made for good airboating conditions. I had never been on an airboat before and was looking forward to it. We met Harry out at the Airboat Association on the Tamiami Trail, Route 41. His boat wasn't much. It looked like a cement-mixing trough with an engine and a seat in it. I think it had a 65 hp airplane motor with a pusher prop. Harry said it could even run on wet grass, but there was plenty of water now.

We put a handful of snake bags, a box, and a couple of snake hooks in the bottom of the boat. Harry hand cranked it and away we went. There was only one seat, so Dad and I stood on either side of that seat and held on for dear life. We had to stand on the snake bags to keep them from being blown into and chewed up by the propeller. One bag as well as my hat had already been mutilated.

The first island/hammock of dry ground was less than a mile out. Most of these hammocks are less than an acre in size, but some are as big as five acres. The Seminole Indians used to live on them and some of them had hunting camps on them.

There were dozens of hammocks in this area. Some of them you could drive right up to them and step right onto dry ground. However, most of them you had to wade to them in waist to chest-high water. Now and then, you would step into a gator hole and be totally submerged. Total immersion was always exciting. You never knew what was going to happen.

This particular island had a hunting cabin on it. In the summer, these cabins were always empty because the mosquitoes were bad during the day and at night so thick, they could carry you away. As I stepped out of the boat, I couldn't believe my eyes. There were snakes everywhere.

King snakes were crawling while mud snakes were under piles of debris. Yellow rat snakes were in the trees and under the shutters of the cabin. Cottonmouth moccasins and pigmy rattlesnakes were crawling everywhere. It was a snake hunter's dream come true or a horrible nightmare for anyone fearful of snakes.

We started bagging snakes left and right. Harry said he had never seen so many snakes in his life, and he had a long lifetime of experiences. The high water had pushed them up onto the high ground. I was having a ball!

Harry took us to a few more islands and they all had snakes on them — lots of them! On some of these hammocks, you could not walk without stepping on a snake.

On another island I had filled the bag with king snakes and was carrying it back to the boat when I saw a large diamondback rattler. I decided to catch it right then before it got into the brush. I pinned the rattler (I don't pin them anymore), and while carrying the kings and this rattler over to the boat, I almost stepped on another big rattlesnake. I put the first rattler in the box with some cottonmouths, went back, and caught the second one.

We decided to dump out a bag of water snakes and fill it with more valuable king and rat snakes. We quickly filled all the bags and the box. We could have caught two or three times as many snakes as we had. We simply had nothing else in which to put them. Nevertheless, it was quite a day. I know I'll never see another day like that again, and I doubt anyone else will either.

We had bags with over 50 pigmy rattlesnakes, 30 king snakes, 30 yellow rat snakes, 20 cottonmouth moccasins, 20 mud snakes, 2 diamondbacks, and an indigo snake. It may seem like over collecting, and it was, but in those days, most people killed every snake on sight. Our snakes went to the pet trade where they would lead less hectic lives.

If the snakes were stuck on these islands for any length of time, there would have been some very fat indigo and king snakes since they are both are snake eaters. We had a nice 40 mph ride back to the landing. The airboat was the only way to get around out there since it was too wet and muddy for a swamp buggy. We bought an airboat shortly after this and had fun with it for years.

Everything went fine until we got back to Davie. As I was dumping the bags into boxes, I got careless. As I picked up the corner of a bag of cottonmouths, one of them got a fang into the first joint of my index finger. Bags with sewn corners would have prevented this.

It really hurt right away, and it seemed to hurt worse if someone looked at it. We probably did all the wrong things by cutting, sucking, and soaking my finger in ice water; although the ice did give me relief from the pain. We didn't think much of doctors in those days since we had seen some poor snake bite treatments and results. At twenty- one, I thought I was tough enough to survive without a doctor's help.

Well, my hand and arm swelled up to my elbow about twice the normal size and turned black, blue, and green. Four or five days later, it started to smell. One night, I had to sleep with my hand out of the window because of the stench. In the morning, we figured I had better get to a hospital and have some part of my hand andor arm cut off.

Dad drove me to a big hospital in Miami. We thought a bigger hospital would be better equipped and have more experience. In the emergency room, I told them the problem. They said to sit down, someone would be with me shortly - you know that line.

There were about 20 other people there, some of them bleeding all over the place. One guy had stuck his hand under a lawnmower and cut off a couple of fingers. A nurse stuck his hand in a basin of disinfectant, and he was getting greener by the minute. Word got around about my snakebite and every few minutes, a couple of doctors would come by, look at my hand, and leave. A few minutes later, a couple more would come by and take a look.

Everyone else just sat there and was hurting. The doctors had never seen a snake bite before and they were sending everyone down to look at it. I was feeling good except for a finger that was rotting away.

A candy striper came by and took my temperature. She was cute and from Saskatoon, Canada. Why she was in Miami was beyond me. She said I had a one-degree above normal temperature. I thought my temperature should have been higher since she was cuter than that. Every time she took my pulse, it increased by five beats.

Finally, a doctor showed up to treat me, the other guy was still bleeding in his basin. He looked, poked, and finally said I had gangrene. It was advancing up my arm and my arm needed to be amputated just below the elbow. He also said more of my arm might have to be amputated in days to come. All this time, he was drawing lines on my arm with his pen.

I asked him if he had ever treated a snakebite before. He said no, but he had studied it in med school. Needless to say, we got out of there in a hurry!

I think Bill Haast of Miami Serpentarium fame recommended a doctor. Bill had had multiple snake bite experiences from extracting venom from poisonous snakes. We went to a Dr. Dunn who had treated many bites in Central America.

He looked at my finger and arm and painted a better picture. Yes, the first joint was dead, but with a few shots, he thought the gangrene would disappear. He said to let the fingertip fall off where and when it wanted to. Dr. Dunn's nurse came in to give me the first shot. I started to roll up my sleeve, but she said, "Drop them!"

Well, I dropped my pants and just as she went to inject me, I tightened up and the needle bent 90 degrees and never went in. On the next try, she pinched me a few times until I relaxed and the shot didn't hurt at all. All future shots from her were preceded by a pinch. One ironic note, as she was treating me to save my hand, her husband had his hand cut off in an airboat accident.

A few days later, there was nothing much left of my fingertip but the skin and nail. The flesh had rotted away, so I took a pair of scissors and cut the skin off. It had been just flopping around and there wasn't any pain. Now the bone was sticking out, so I pulled on it a little. It came loose and fell off.

I put both of my fingertip remnants in a bottle of alcohol and I still have them. I was kind of attached to them at one time.

After a couple of weeks of shots and several months, the skin finally grew over the end of the second joint. My finger never received any stitches. It was very sensitive for a few years but is fine now. I even type with my short finger. About the only problem I have now is shooting a handgun. I now need one with a small grip or I have to shoot single action. This was the only bad bite I have ever had, and it made me more careful.

My parents and I were working for the summer in the Adirondacks of New York. We were at a tourist attraction called the Adirondack Sportsman Show. We were the entire show. We did fishing and shooting demonstrations as well as animal and snake acts.

My cousin Doug and I used to go fishing at a nearby brook. We brought back live trout in plastic bags and put them in a pool in the show's arena. This pool also doubled as an alligator pool. During the show, we would tie a live moth onto a fishing rod and drop it into the pool. A trout would take it every time and this really impressed the audience.

I was sixteen at the time, and I did the snake handling. I had some copperhead and timber rattlers that I had gotten from Rattlesnake Nick Nichols, a snake hunting companion of the famous herpetologist, Carl Kauffeld.

One of the copperheads was pretty tame and I took too many liberties with it. I went to get this snake from the pit and picked it up free-hand and started to carry it the 50 feet to the arena. It got jumpy and I dropped it. I looked for my snake hook, but it was missing. About then the snake started to crawl behind some boxes and I reached down, grabbed it by the tail to flip it into the open.

As I flipped it, it turned and got one fang in the meaty side of my hand. It didn't hurt much, but I put a garbage can over the snake and went to the arena where my father was performing. I told him what had happened, found the snake hook, went back, and got the snake. I finished the snake show and then Dad, never one to miss an opportunity, brought me back into the arena.

He explained to the 50 people watching what had happened. Then he took his knife and made an incision and sucked some blood out. I doused my hand with antiseptic and returned to the arena. Some guy came up and said it was a very interesting show. He wondered if we did the snakebite "thing" every show.

I didn't have much problem from that bite. My hand swelled up a little and was sore for a week, but that was all. I don't think anyone ever died from a copperhead bite, but they are nothing to fool around with. You never know, you could be the unlucky first.

I used to meet a lot of guys out hunting and they would come by the house now and then to talk snakes. One guy phoned me to say he was at the hospital because he had been bitten on his ankle by a small cottonmouth. He had not told anyone since he had felt fine. However, while putting his shorts on for gym class two days later, he saw his leg was black and blue up to his groin. The coach quickly took him to the hospital. When the doctors discussed amputating his leg, he called me.

I told him to call Dr. Ben Shepard and Bill Haast, both snakebite experts. They both went to the hospital, suggested the best treatment and the boy's leg turned out as good as new. So, make sure you get a second opinion on anything serious, especially snakebites.

Scarlet Kingsnakes

In Davie, Florida, my parents and I lived in a little house on Flamingo Road. It was a quiet country road with a canal between the road and our house. Later, a drainpipe was put in the canal and filled in around it. All the roadside trees were also cut down. That quiet road was turned into a six-lane high-speed road that no snake could ever safely cross. But more than 40 years ago, Flamingo road was nice and peaceful.

The good stretch of road was only about three miles long and the road was lined with Australian pine trees. These pines were 50 to 100 feet tall and at times full of corn snakes and scarlet king snakes. I used to be able to cross the little bridge, walk along the trees and catch anywhere from one to ten scarlet kings almost any night. A corn or yellow rat snake could usually be found also.

In the daytime, you could catch corns and yellows and now and then an indigo. By peeling the bark from dead trees, you could find scarlet kings, corn and yellow rat snakes.

I wasn't working regularly then and these snakes kept a few dollars in my pocket. In truth, catching snakes was the only thing I wanted to do. Snakes weren't worth much in those days, but things didn't cost much either. Today, I get twice as much for a small bag of snakes as I used to get for five big bags full. It was no problem for three or four guys hunting together to catch 40 to 50 snakes in a few hours. I'm talking good size snakes, too.

In the twenty years I hunted that area, I never saw a poisonous coral snake. This took all the worry out of grabbing a tri-color that was crawling through the grass. Where I live now, all three tri-colors - the coral, the scarlet king and scarlet snake - are found, and when they are moving, they all look alike.

My cousin Don Offen and his wife Rosemary were one evening. I said I was going snake hunting and. Rosemary wanted to go along. Don told us not to be long for he wanted to leave soon. I knew we could probably catch one in a few minutes right in front of the house.

Rosemary wasn't a snake person, but she was interested in seeing how I caught them. With a couple of flashlights, we started walking along the road. In minutes, I found two scarlet kings and then two more.

"Boy," Rosemary said, "it's easy to catch snakes!" We returned to keep Don happy and found two more snakes right where we had just been.

The Offens left, and I told Dad that the scarlet kings were crawling. He grabbed a light and went the opposite way along the road. I drove a half-mile down the road and caught six more. When I got back, Dad had five for a grand total of seventeen scarlet kings in an hour.

It was a very profitable evening. Today, the dealers pay around $50 a piece for what was a $5 snake in those days.

Here's a little tip that might be helpful if you are ever night hunting for snakes. Scarlet kings eat skinks. Now skinks only come out in the daytime, so if you are walking along and see a skink running around in the dark, wait there a few minutes. Often, a scarlet king or a corn snake is following right behind it.

Road Hunting Tricks

When you know you are going to snake hunt a certain road, drive it beforehand and throw all the trash off the road. It's amazing how much a fan belt looks like a snake at night. I have almost wrecked my car stopping to try and catch one of those rare yellow banana peel snakes.

Once someone had peeled an orange in a spiral and had thrown it out the window. I was sure I had seen one of those peels start to crawl. I was wrong.

Another time, watermelons were being packed in trucks with shredded newspapers to keep them from being bruised. As the melon trucks drove down the road, some of the paper would blow onto the highway. The colored comic shreds looked just like the milk snakes and drove us crazy. We finally had to go to another road that didn't have any paper snakes.

Out alone the road there used to be a lot of inner tubes from cars and trucks. They became great snake hideouts. When we found a whole tube, we would cut a hole so the snakes could crawl in.

Today we have tubeless tires, so snakes have lost these hideouts. We often caught two or three kinds of snakes in one tube. For some reason, when I first started hunting in south

Florida, we would take the tube and dump it into the other guys hands. That worked fine until someone dumped a cottonmouth in my hand! After that we just dumped the snakes onto the ground and had plenty of time to catch them. You might miss a racer, but not a king or yellow rat snake.

The following is a trick that won't help you catch snakes but might make you a few enemies. I bought some rubber snakes and set them on a road my buddy was going to cruise one night. When we returned that night, each in our own car, I was surprised when he said nothing about rubber snakes. There were a couple of other snake hunters at the motel and we were comparing our catches. They had a CB radio and one of their friends who was still road cruising came on and said he would kill the guy who put the rubber snakes on the road. The guy talking said he was almost killed saving a rubber snake from a ten-wheeler. Needless to say, I told no one about my little joke.

Lots of Water Snakes

One year it was very dry in South Florida and there were a lot of fires in the Everglades. There was a large area that burned on the east side of State Road 27, below Hollywood Boulevard. On the west side was a large canal.

All the snakes on the east side had all the cover burned off, so they were crawling across the high-way to get to the water on the other side of the road.

The problem was that the highway was quite busy. I found the snakes on the way back from a rattlesnake hunting trip. There were hundreds of them dead on the road along a five-mile stretch of highway. I went back the next afternoon and caught about a hundred. They started to crawl late in the afternoon and continued for about three hours.

The next evening, my rodeo buddy Guy Quail and I went out to the same place and they were really crawling good. There were thousands of them dead on the road and they piled up smelling badly.

We started walking along the side of the road, and we couldn't pick them up fast enough. We were walking stooped over with a bag in one hand and picking them up with the other. It was just like picking up fallen apples.

When the bag got heavy, we'd go back to the car, get another bag, and drive ahead a little. We started running out of bags, so we were dumping one bag into another then adding more and tying them with string because the knots took up too much space. The bags were 100-pound grain bags just to give you an idea of how many snakes we had.

Finally, just at dark, we found two corn snakes and fitted them in as they were worth more. We weren't carrying any lights because we didn't have enough hands. Most of the waters were two to three footers. Just as we were getting back into the car with totally stuffed bags, I saw a large snake in the headlights of an oncoming car. It didn't look quite right, so I waited until another car came along and saw that it was a large cottonmouth. I'm glad I didn't just grab it like I did all the others. We didn't have anything to put it in, so we dragged it off the road with a stick and left it for another day.

We had nine bags FULL. We counted one bag and estimated we had around 800 water snakes and two corn snakes. Not a bad night's work and most of them would have been run over. We took them down to the Miami Serpentarium owned by Bill Haast. I think he paid ten cents apiece and he didn't make a good count, he just estimated. All in all, it was an experience that I will never have again.

A few days later, they stopped crawling, but it sure smelled out there for a while!

Someone, many years ago, wrote that you could drive out from Miami on the Tamiami Trail, Route 41, slam on your brakes, and slide all the way to Naples, Florida, about 100 miles, on the backs of dead snakes. And it is almost true!

Route 27

You never knew what you might find when snake hunting along Route 27 in Broward and Palm Beaches Counties. One day I was walking the shoulder of the road right along the mowed edge where it was easy walking. Between the swamp and the mowed area were four feet of thick grass and bushes. That's where most of the snakes were. On the other side of the highway, there were 15 to 20 feet of dry land and then a wide canal.

Both sides possessed snakes, but one side or the other would be better depending on the weather or the time of year. On this day, I was on the west swamp side when I saw a large mud snake crawling through the grass. It looked unusually long, too long. Picking it up, I saw not one snake, but four. There were three, four-foot males mating with a six-foot female. As she was crawling, she dragged the three males behind her. It must have been very uncomfortable for all of them. I gently put them in a bag and continued on. They were still coupled the next day, but they separated that evening. Unfortunately, I didn't get a picture. I've always regretted not taking more pictures of things like that. It was a once in a lifetime opportunity.

On another day I found a couple of pieces of tin that had fallen off a truck. Tin is great for the snakes to get under, so I dragged it off to a dry spot in the swamp and spread out the pieces. I caught a few snakes under them off and on over the years and then I forgot about those pieces. One day, a few years later, I was out hunting and remembered the tin, so I waded out to it. The bushes had grown up, but I found it.

One piece was in the sun and too hot. The other was nice and shady but covered with vines. I cut the many vines with my knife in order to lift it. Upon picking it up, it was solid with mud snakes. They scoop holes out, lay their eggs, and coil around them until they hatch. There were eight mud snakes, one very fat king snake, and about 200 eggs.

The king was full of snake eggs it had made under there. There had been more mud snakes and eggs under the tin, but raccoons had reached under the edges and pulled them out for supper. The depressions where the nests had been could still be seen. I bagged the snakes and the eggs as the raccoons would have eaten them now that the vines were loosened.

I hatched all the eggs and turned all the neonates, baby snakes, loose as they had no value. A mud snake is quite pretty, shiny black and red, although I have caught black and white ones. They lack personality and are difficult to feed, but they never bite.

Recently I went back out to this area after a long absence. Luckily, I found where someone had placed some tin along the canal bank. There were typically two pieces of tin with a rock on top. I have found eight tin groups along a three-mile stretch of highway. They looked like they were put out from a boat, as they were hard to see from the road. I have caught ten kings under them in the last year. I guess kings are coming back a little and I certainly will not catch them all.

Robbers

One fall day I was out along State Road 27, just below Andytown (it's now a huge housing development), I was bird hunting for a Wilson's Snipe (Jack Snipe) instead of hunting snakes. I don't snake hunt all the time, it just seems like it!

Snipe are probably the most difficult to hit of any game bird, as they seldom fly more than a few feet in the same direction, constantly zigging and zagging. There has been many a time that I have seen my shot hit six feet one side or to the other because it zigged just as I shot.

I know lots of people who would shoot a whole box of 25 shells and only get a few birds. My best day was 8 birds, the limit, with 9 shots — almost perfect, but I had to shoot one twice.

I had parked right along the highway and walked across the road out into the swamp. It was pretty open with small clumps of sawgrass and willows growing in only a little water but deep mud. The snipe eat worms and there were lots of worms and lots of birds. I was jump shooting with no dog. Another bird got up which I had shot and then it dropped right into a little clump of sawgrass. I started to put my hand in to pick it up when I saw that it was lying right on top of a fairly large cottonmouth. That moccasin would have gotten me for sure if I had reached in without looking.

I pinned it with the butt of the shotgun and put it into a bag which I always carry. That bird had been number seven, and I got one more on the way back to the car for my limit. I cut over to the road instead of heading directly to the car because the mud was hard to walk in. I came out about 150 yards from my car. The road level was built up about four feet above the water because the swamp water got pretty high. I was on the side of the road opposite my car. It was a two-lane road then.

I had my shotgun unloaded and I was knocking the mud off my boots. Looking up the road, I noticed a car parked right across from mine. I knew it wasn't there a few minutes ago. I couldn't see my car very well from where I was, but then I saw the top of a guy's head by my car.

Well, I dropped a couple of double O buck shells into the shotgun, grabbed the cottonmouth, and started trotting down low toward my car. I got about 50 yards away when they saw me. I was on the same side of the road as their car and it was facing me. They flew across the road, jumped in, and started the car. They didn't have anything in their hands, or I might have done something differently.

They didn't have time to turn around because I was too close. They came right at me, but on the wrong side of the road. I was standing in the middle of the road. It's amazing the options that went through my mind in just a couple of seconds: shoot the driver, shoot the passenger (he was closer), shoot the engine, tires, or windshield, or all of the above. I couldn't have missed any of them or the car. They were ducking and screaming as they went by and I fired both barrels over their heads. They almost wrecked and I bet there were a couple of WET spots on their seats when they got home. I bet they will think twice before they try to break into another car; or, at least, make sure there isn't a big crazy guy standing in the middle of the road with a great big gun!

They had managed to get the door open without breaking anything and had just started to take my tape player out when I arrived. They don't know how lucky they were, but I did come out ahead with a nice new screwdriver as a souvenir. Even today I'm still mad I didn't shoot them just on general principles.

Tarzan

A buddy of mine, his girlfriend, and her sister came by one day to visit and look at our cougars, deer and bears. I showed them around and we had a good time. A few days later, the sister, Vivian, came by again. Just down from New York, she wanted to take a ride out to the Everglades. She had never been there, and I liked the Everglades because of all the reptiles we might find. It was less than ten miles to Andytown, which no longer exists, on Route 27. In those days, it was typical Everglades, water, heat, humidity, trees, and wildlife.

I parked at a boat-launching ramp and we watched the huge flocks of birds flying by. Unfortunately, many of these large flocks don't exist anymore due to so much construction in south Florida. Just recently, I saw a flock of about fifty ibis fly by, so there may be hope.

I just happened to have a small bottle of wine and a few cokes in a cooler in case we got marooned. I do not drink, but I took a few sips of wine to be sociable. After a while, we decided to go back but I was a little dizzy. I said, "Let's walk around so I can clear my head, and maybe we can find a snake." Vivian was a New Yorker and not too keen on snakes but game anyway.

We walked along the road and came to some Australian pine trees. I looked up and saw a yellow rat snake about forty feet up a skinny tree.

"How are you going to catch it?" she asked.

"Easy," I said, "I'll shimmy right up the tree." I was in good shape then. I caught the snake, but I did not have a bag. I usually put it in my tee shirt in these situations, but I had on a button shirt. I decided the heck with it since I was still a little high from the wine, so I just held the snake in one hand and leaned out holding the tree with the other. The tree bent over and lowered me right to the ground at Vivian's feet. I let go of the tree and it straightened back up.

I do not know why the tree did not break and drop me on my head. Anyway, I have not had a drink since. I do not know if I impressed Vivian, but she did call me Tarzan for quite a while.

No Trick

I was out snake hunting on Route 27 with my buddy Bill Sargent. We were north of the Everglades up along the sugarcane fields.

I can see why the old farmers wanted to drain the Everglades, the soil was beautiful. When the fields were just plowed, it looked like ground up chocolate cake. In some places, the dirt was fifteen to twenty feet deep, an accumulation of hundreds of years of dead grass and plants.

We were hunting right along the highway and the plowed fields came right up to the right of way. The fields went as far as the eye could see with just a narrow strip of cover along the road. Here is where the snakes could be found.

I had parked at a likely spot and we decided to split up to cover more ground. Bill started walking north and I went south. I would walk about fifteen minutes and cross over to the other side and walk back to the car. I would then drive to my partner, pick up any snakes that he had, and start over again. At times, one side of the road was more productive than the other and we would hunt mostly that side.

Once, as I drove to pick up Bill, I happened to look out at the plowed field. There right out in the open was a very large yellow rat snake stretched out on this nice brownish-black soil. You would have had to be blind not to see it.

I parked on the opposite side and started out after it. I was about fifty yards out when I stopped. Now, Bill has been known to pull a few pranks. He had gotten me many times and this was so obvious, I knew it had to be one of Bill's tricks. I was not going to walk all the way over there only to find out it was a dead snake Bill had found on the road and placed it where I would see it. I was congratulating myself for not being fooled when I happened to look at the dead snake and it was crawling. I was the one that was almost fooled. The snake was fine, but I do not know what on earth it was doing out in the middle of the open field. You catch them where you find them.

I drove, picked up Bill, and we caught a few more yellow snakes and some nice king snakes. We had a great time and I did not get fooled again.

A Mud Snake Bonanza

I took the old airboat out one day, it was just like a big cement mixing trough with a sixty-five horse power Continental aircraft motor and a gas tank, but it ran. Skeet Johns was along to keep me out of trouble. We launched at the Blue Shanty west of Miami along Route 41 and headed south. There are lots of little islands/hammocks all around there, but if you go too far southwest, you hit the Everglades National Park where you cannot hunt.

We stopped at some islands and caught a few snakes. Then we came to an island with a lot of cabbage palm trees. As the leaves, fronds, fall off they make quite a bit of trash under the trees. Using our snake sticks, we dug through the leaves and started pulling out some big mud snakes. They were up to six feet long and had clumps of eggs. The muds scoop out a place in the dirt and coil around the eggs until they hatch. They never bite but I guess their presence keeps predators away. I don't know why as it does not work on people.

We came back with 28 big muds and over 600 eggs. We could not leave the eggs because the raccoons would have eaten them in a few days.

I had eggs in everything coffee cans, gallon jars and some vegetable crispers from a couple of dead refrigerators. Almost every one of the eggs hatched and there were a few baby kings and yellow rat snakes in there too. We did catch a few very fat king snakes under the leaves that were gorging on the mud snake eggs.

I ended up turning most of the babies loose. I found out the guy to whom I was selling them to was pickling the eggs for dissection or something. I do not like selling them to be killed if I can help it.

More Garter Snakes

I was out on Route 27 again, walking along the canal side, where the shoulder was twenty to thirty feet wide. I was catching a few odd snakes but nothing special, when I came to an area with a lot of clumps of heavy grass. All of a sudden, the ground and the grass were crawling with garter snakes. I had never seen so many at one time in one place.

There had to be at least a hundred and they were going in a hundred different directions. I started grabbing and got a pretty good bag full before they scattered. It seemed like it was a den, but I had never heard of a den in south Florida. It could have also been the start or the end of a mating frenzy.

As I continued walking ahead, I picked up a few more garter snakes. Then five or six garters came crawling towards me. They looked like they were being chased and I was right. Two big king snakes came crawling right behind them. Naturally, I caught the two kings and as I was putting them in the bag, I saw a commotion in the grass ahead of me.

When I walked up, there was another king eating a garter snake. When I picked the king up, it dropped the garter snake which crawled away thanking its lucky stars. The garters must have thought they were between a rock and a hard place. King snakes on one side and me on the other. All in all, it was a pretty wild few minutes, and I have never seen it like that again.

Too Close Alligator

My alligator wrestling friend Tommy Taylor got a call from a man in Davie, Florida one day. The man said an alligator had eaten both his cats and had just missed catching his dog. He wanted Tommy to come and remove it.

Tommy and I went out a lot catching nuisance gators and snakes or whatever. We had permits from the state, now there are licensed trappers. We would relocate them, or Tommy would use some of them in his wrestling shows.

I put our little johnboat on top of the car and met Tommy down at the man's house. He lived on a large rock-pit. It was three or four hundred feet over to the other side of the pond. It was night at dark when we arrived. I shined my light around a little and saw two red eyes glowing way over on the other side.

"This should be easy," I remembered thinking. I gave a few grunts aka gator talk just out of habit. Some gators will come to a call but not too often.

We spent a few minutes getting our gear together: fishing rod, ropes, noose, and large rubber bands for its jaw. I got my headlight on and we slid the boat into the water. I turned my light on and looked over on the opposite bank where I had first seen the gator, but there was nothing.

"Maybe we had a spooky one," I thought. I looked all around and still no red glowing eyes. Then I saw something move right alongside of the boat. Looking down, there was a seven-foot alligator right alongside of us. We had not even started to paddle yet. The gator had come all the way across to meet us.

I had the rod with the weighted treble hook in my hand, but the gator was too close. I did not have room to cast, but I didn't need to. When I got my wits back, I just let a little line out, got the hook alongside of the gator, and snagged it.

After a short fight, we got a noose around its neck and dragged it up the bank. We tied it up and loaded it into Tommy's truck. It was one of the fastest catches I had ever made. We were starting to load everything up when the man came out of his house and asked why we were leaving.

I said, "We caught it already."

The man said he could not believe it, as he had just gone into the house for a few minutes to tell his wife something.

I said, "We're fast!"

I think he wanted us to turn it loose and catch it again so could watch. HA!

Tommy Taylor & Frank Weed wrangling a crocodile

Gordon Johnston

Gordon (Gordy) Johnston has been gone for over forty years now, but I still remember him well. Gordy influenced many young snake hunters and put them on the right path.

He looked me up one Christmas day about 1960. He had four guys with him on a collecting trip. It had been too cold in the Carolinas, so they continued to south Florida. Someone had mentioned my name to them, so five snow birds showed up in my yard hoping to go herping aka snake hunting.

One of the guys was Dick Bartlett, today famous for the many reptile books and articles he has written. Another herper was Syd Chapin, who I still go collecting with today some forty-five years later. I don't remember what we found but I think they were happy!

Gordon came down a while later, probably Easter vacation since he was a teacher in New Jersey. He wanted a scarlet king snake and wondered if I could find one. I said I probably could as I had been catching quite a few. He said he had only caught three or four in his entire life.

It was late afternoon and the scarlet kings don't show themselves until after dark. To kill some time, we walked the

Australian pine tree line along Flamingo Road and caught some rat snakes— red and yellows. Gordon was elated.

As darkness fell, we drove over to a little dirt road that was usually pretty snakey. There were Australian pines here also. These pines were wanted back in the early thirties and were good for birds nesting and the rat snakes that liked their eggs and hatchlings. Today, these pines are considered a nuisance and are being removed in many places.

To catch scarlet kings, all you need is a light, a bag, and the rig area. I had the first two items and felt we were in the right place, so I got out and walked around to Gordy's side of the car and switched on my light. He was getting his stuff ready.

I asked, "Are you ready yet'

He said, "Almost."

I said, "Don't take too long. There is a scarlet king right by your foot."

He sure found his light in a hurry. He then almost missed it, he was so excited. We found SIX more in the next hour until rain began and sent the snakes underground. This time I knew he was happy.

Another time Gordy arrived with a sixteen-year-old named Ray Van Nostrand, present owner of Strictly Reptiles. Their quest this time was for an indigo snake, they were legal to catch then. Unlike the scarlet king, I wasn't as confident about an indigo but knew a few places we could look. In short, I promised nothing. So off we went to a little dirt road about two miles away where I had previous success. Along this road was a small canal quite overgrown.

We hadn't gone half a block when Ray made a flying leap into the bushes and emerged with a beautiful five-foot indigo, his first ever. He was so excited I thought he would fly away. We went another fifty yards and Ray jumped into the bushes and caught another indigo.

Another hundred yards and Ray caught his third, a big six-footer this time. Gordon and I caught nothing, we were having too much fun watching him. A few minutes later, we found a big five-foot diamondback rattler. I decided to catch it since Ray was really keyed up and I was afraid he might get careless. All in all, it was a great little hunt.

Gordy always stopped by anytime he was in my area. He was a good friend and hunting companion and I miss him.

A Cold Piece of Tin

My friend John Kemnitzer said that even if he was in the Arctic and he found a piece of tin on the ground he would look under it for snakes. I am the same way.

One day I was in Gainesville, Florida visiting my friend Bob Kromer. There was some property down the road that he was thinking of buying, and he wanted me to go with him to look at it. It was very cold that morning, frost all over everything, not good snake hunting weather. I took a bag and my snake stick along anyway, you never know. We walked around awhile looking the place over when we came upon a shed from which a couple of pieces of tin had fallen off.

They were lying on the ground totally coated with frost. I started to walk over to the tin, when Bob said, "Don't bother, there won't be anything under that cold piece of tin."

Well, leave no piece of tin unturned I always say. I couldn't leave it without looking, so I went over and lifted it. There was a nice diamondback lying there. What a surprise! There wasn't a hole under it so the snake couldn't go any deeper. I lifted it with my hook, and it was so cold it could not rattle, just click, click, click was all it could do. It was so stiff that I knew it could not strike, so I just reached down and picked it up and dropped it in the bag without a problem.

Bob about had a fit: look out, be careful, all that kind of stuff. He catches snakes too, but he is a lot more careful than I am and that is why he has never been bitten. I am really more careful than it looks, but I like to get Bob's goat sometimes. All the way back to the car, we walked to the tune of click, click, click. It was a nice sound to a snake hunter especially on a cold morning.

State Road 27

At one time, State Road 27 had more snakes along it than any other place I've ever seen. There were times when you could just walk along the side of the shoulder of the road and catch all the snakes you could carry. Good varieties too, kings and yellow rats mostly but also diamondbacks, cottonmouths, garters, waters, and green snakes.

Many times, I would see the yellow bellies of the keeled green snakes in the second growth Australian pines while driving. If there was only one or two, I would drive until there were three or four close together so I wouldn't have to walk too far. There were times when I would catch 30 or 40 greens in a few hours plus all the other snakes I could find. Every day was not great but most of them were.

The highway ran north and south. On the right, going north, was a big canal with a row of Australian pines between the road and the canal. The left side was all Everglades for about 40 miles. The trees were full of yellow rat snakes and green snakes. The kings were on the ground on both sides where there were breaks in the trees. Waters and cottonmouths were everywhere. Many days I would fill all my bags and have to leave the rest for another day.

Typically, I would drive to a likely looking spot and park on the side of the road. If I was alone, I would walk for three or four blocks or until the bags got heavy, cross to the other side and walk back to the car. There was only a narrow strip, from ten to thirty feet wide, of dry ground to look in. It was very easy hunting. Dropping off whatever I had caught at the car, I would walk back the opposite way and repeat, then drive ahead one-half mile and do the same.

If I had someone that had ridden with me, I would drop them along the road, drive ahead a half mile ahead, and park. The other guy would hunt to the car and drive up to me. We would keep skipping along like that until we got tired, sometimes six or more miles a day. There were days when two guys would catch 15 to 20 kings, 20 to 30 yellows and dozens of lesser critters. This was all in the 1960's.

Nowadays, there are still a few snakes out there but almost all the trees have been cut down and most of the swamp has been drained for sugarcane. The road is now four-lanes and herbicide is sprayed alone the right-of-way to keep the bushes down. I still go out there once in a while, just for old times' sake, but many times I don't see a snake. It's a little sad!

A Snake Lover He Wasn't

One day I was out hunting along Route 27 where I was doing very good. I had bags and bags full of king snakes and lots of other critters. As I got back to my car, a State Trooper stopped to check on me. There wasn't much traffic in those days. Talking for a while, he indicated he did not like snakes much, but he was interested in them. I showed him some of the snakes I had caught, and he even touched one.

"Maybe I have a convert here," I was thinking.

As he went to leave, he said, "Be careful and drive carefully because if you get in a wreck, I am not going to drag you out of a car full of snakes!"

Frank and a van full of snakes

Four-Lined Skinks

I was out hunting along Route 27 in Palm Beach County one day. I was catching a few assorted snakes, kings and yellows mostly, and I was always looking for four-lined skinks, blue-tailed skinks because they were younger, since that was all my Mexican milk snake would eat. It would not touch an anole which were very common and easy to get.

As I walked along, I came to a place where there had been an accident. A dump truck had rolled over and lost its load of nice white sand. It had been there for some time, but I never paid it much attention. It was fairly cool out, but not cold. A few people had taken advantage of the accident and hauled away some of the sand. Anyway, there was this big mound of sand with a deep depression in the middle almost like a crater in a volcano about five feet deep.

I jumped in, dug in the side with my snake hook and a couple of skinks came tumbling out. They were kind of holed up during the cool weather. The sand was nice and dry, and it was easy to dig into.

If you have ever tried to catch skinks, you know how fast they are. But in this hole, they could not get going and they were easy to catch. I would just reach up and pull-down part of the rim and two or three would drop down into the hole. I would catch those and do it again. I got over fifty in just a little while. I knew my milk snake would be happy for a long time. I have never found them like that again, two or three under a board but that's about it.

Australian Pine Trees and Yellow Rats

I do not know the guy's name who authorized the planting of the Australian pine trees along many of the roads in South Florida, but he did the snake population a big favor. The guy that had them removed hurt the snakes a lot. They planted lots of them around the orange groves to buffer storm damage and the snakes liked them.

Forty years ago, a snake could crawl from Lake Okeechobee to Fort Lauderdale without touching the ground (80 or 90 miles). Now there are only a few scattered trees left on Route 27. There used to be trees along Route 41 from the Miami city limits all the way past Forty-Mile Bend and also down Krome Avenue. These were good places for snakes for a long time.

These trees get very dense and up to one hundred feet tall and are the home to all kinds of beasties but especially the yellow rat snake. There used to be thousands of yellows along Route 27. After the trees went, so did the snakes.

I can see why they got rid of the trees along the roads as they were very brittle and during a storm or a hurricane, they came down all over the roads. I counted over one hundred trees down in less than one mile after one storm.

When it was still good, I caught 27 yellows on Route 27 by myself. I finally got tired of climbing trees. I would climb a tree after a yellow snake and look over to the next tree and there would be another one. After catching ten or twelve, I started getting tired. I knew there had to be a better way to catch these yellows. I happened to find a bamboo pole lying along the road and I had a brainstorm. I had apiece of heavy wire in the car, and I made a hook and taped it to the bamboo pole.

Walking along the trees again, I found a yellow stretched out on a limb about fifteen feet over my head. Easing the hook near the snake, I pulled down quickly on the branch and the snake dropped right into my hand, saving me a lot of climbing. If you did not flip the snake off the limb the first time, it usually wrapped around the limb and you had to climb up after it. I have caught hundreds of yellows with the hook.

In the pines that died there were always lots of rotten spots. I used to carry a jack handle or large screwdriver to pry off the dead bark and wood. One day, I pried off a large piece of bark and there were eight large yellow rat snakes in a hole behind it. Two of them were over six feet long.

As the trees started to thin out, the king snakes became more common. Kings like more light. One day by myself, I caught fifteen kings, but that did not happen often. A lot of the swamp are sugarcane fields now. These fields are liked by the king snakes, but it is hard to get permission to hunt there. I heard that a couple of guys got permission last year and caught twenty-three kings in just a little while. At least it is good to know there are still some out there.

Pop Top King Snake

This tale might be a little odd, but it is the way I saw it. While out hunting along Route 27, I came upon a three-foot king snake that had managed to crawl into a pop-top ring from a beverage can. Nowadays, the rings stay on the can. The ring was about halfway down its body.

The snake's body was raw at this spot. It must have been very uncomfortable to crawl or eat, but the king wasn't in that bad of shape yet. I couldn't sell the snake in that condition, but I couldn't leave it in that shape either.

I took it back to the car where I had a pair of wire cutters. With the cutter, I cut the ring off and set the snake in the grass. It started to crawl away, then it stopped, turned toward me, nodded its head up and down as if to say "thank you." Then it turned and crawled away!

I'll always remember that.

Wasps

I was out snake hunting with a buddy one day along the orange groves. In this area, the orange trees were surrounded by a row of Australian pine trees. These were planted to slow down the wind from the hurricanes as they grew fast and got quite tall. However, they were brittle, but they gave me a great place to snake hunt. The snakes loved them because as the trees got older and died, they made good places for the snakes to hide and to lay eggs. I once found over one hundred rat snake eggs in one hollow spot.

We were mostly peeling bark that day which entails digging in the rotten wood. I usually carried a large screwdriver or a jack handle to pry off the bark and pieces of dead wood. We were catching a few snakes, mostly reds and yellows and a few scarlet kings. These trees were spaced about twenty feet apart and there were hundreds of them.

At one large dead tree, I saw some good-looking dead spots about twenty feet up the tree. I decided to climb up, but it was a hard tree to climb as there were not many limbs down low. Finally, I made it up to a strong limb with a boost from my buddy. There was a nice loose piece of bark, about two-foot square just over my head. I reached up and gave a pull. It came loose and about fifty big black wasps that were under it dropped down on me.

The next thing I remembered was being on the ground running away from the tree and the wasps. My buddy said that I flew out of the tree, but I don't remember flapping my arms. I did not get hurt or stung somehow, and I did not go back up that tree. The rest of the day, I was very careful, and I would jump every time a bug flew by.

Dragline Indigo

I was driving out to one of my favorite snake hunting spots on a little backcountry road when I came upon one of the county dragline crews cleaning the hyacinths out of the canal. The dragline was mounted on the back of a truck and the driver would move the truck ahead as needed. The dragline had a perforated bucket on the cable that the operator would swing through the canal. The water would run through the holes and the plants would remain in the bucket to be dumped along the side of the canal and picked up later by another crew. Some of the canals were completely blocked by the plants.

The guy doing the digging this time was the husband of the woman I worked for, so I stopped to say hello. Carlton knew I caught snakes and when I went over, he said that a couple of scoops ago he had dug an indigo snake out of the bank, and it had swum across the 15-foot wide canal. It was fairly open on the other side with just a few bushes.

He said, "Hop in the bucket and I'll swing you across." I did and he did. I got out and right under the first bush was the indigo. I picked it up, they never bite, put it in a bag, got back in the bucket, and he swung me back over. How's that for service?

The Knack or Lack of Knack

A friend of the family was out visiting us one day. We were sitting around talking and I said I was going snake hunting for a while. He asked if he could ride along and I agreed since I liked company. We only went about five miles when we noticed a lot of fresh dead snakes on the road. We figured this was a good place to start. I parked along the road and we started walking the shoulder of the road. There were snakes everywhere but just mostly garter snakes and water snakes. You catch what is crawling, some are just worth more than others.

I was catching them left and right. I'd just pick them up and put them in a bag. My friend finally said that it looked easy and wanted to try.

"Be my guest," I said. He picked one up and the garter promptly bit him. I caught about ten more and none bit me.

"Let me try again," my friend said. He picked up another garter and it bit him again. Some people just have the knack or lack of knack. I am very seldom ever bitten.

A few days later in that same area, I caught 76 snakes in a little over an hour, mostly garters and waters, but a few kings and yellow rats and a couple of cottonmouths. The radio was playing "Seventy-six Trombones" so it made it easy to remember. Of all those snakes, I had gotten only one or two water snake bites.

$$$$$$$

I was out snake hunting one day after work by just walking along the highway. I was catching a few odd snakes but nothing special. I considered going home when I saw a one-dollar bill lying in the grass.

Most of the snakes in those days were only worth a dollar or less so it was just as good as catching a snake but not as much fun. Walking further, there was another dollar, then another and another things were getting interesting. Then I found a twenty-dollar bill and I really got interested. I went back and forth on both sides of the road, but it got dark and I did not find anything else.

The next day at work I could hardly wait for my workday to end. At quitting time, I jumped into my car and headed back out to the same place. I started looking and there was another twenty-dollar bill. This was fun. All this money and I did not even have to drive into town to sell the snakes. As I continued walking, I thought to myself, if I were a twenty-dollar bill where would I go? Well, there was a bush on the edge of the road, and I thought I would blow under there. I lifted the bush with my hook and there was a nice big diamondback rattlesnake.

It wasn't worth twenty dollars back then, but that was all right with me.

Caiman Catching

A good buddy, Guy Quail (we rodeoed together in South America), and I got a tip that there were some wild caiman, South American alligators, in a canal in North Miami. So, we went down one evening to check it out. Alligators were protected then, but caiman were not.

They do not get as big as alligators, but they are fun to catch, and I could sell them. Even though they were not worth much, we just liked the thrill of the chase.

We found the area which was right in the middle of a residential park with houses all around, I said there cannot be much here with all these people, but when I shined a light down a small canal, the water lit up like a Christmas tree from all the caiman eyes. They glow bright red.

The canal was about 20 feet wide and five feet deep. The canal was a little too deep to wade and besides it was full of hydrilla weed right up to the top. Guy went down one side of the canal and I took the other. The grass was too thick for the rod and hook, so we just grabbed most of them.

A lot of caimans went under the grass, but we managed to catch about twenty, mostly babies but a few were three footers. They have one quirk that is their undoing. Whenever you shined a light on them, they would sink straight down and you could go right where you last saw them, stick your hand down, grab them and you would have them…most of the time anyway. Crocodiles act the same way, but alligators go down, take off, and come up 50 to 100 feet away. Once you figure out how they react, it is easy.

I used to go back now and then and there were always a few, but they are now putting pipes in the canals. They plan to put houses there, so there will not be too many caimans anymore. I had heard that someone had some caiman in a cage in back of his house and that it had escaped during a hurricane.

They sure did well there for quite a while. We caught a few over four feet at other times. One night, I was on a footbridge over one of the larger canals with my heavy gator rod. Suddenly a caiman that had to be seven feet popped up right in front of me. I got so excited that when I went to cast, I got a backlash. My perfect shot with no trees, just open water was ruined. This one did take off and I never saw it again. It would not be fun if you got them all.

I was alone one night without a boat and I saw a couple of caimans on the other side of the small canal. There wasn't any way to walk around so I just waded into the four-foot deep canal. I swung the battery to the headlamp to the back of my neck. I got across and caught a few caiman, but on the way back, I found a deep spot up to my neck. Now the canal was full of duckweed, small floating plants only one fourth of an inch wide. It has roots about one inch long and it completely covered the surface. So, when I came out, it completely covered me. I looked like I was wearing a green blanket. Just then one of the local police officers pulled up and gave me a strange look. I was standing there dripping and removing this green stuff from every inch of my body. I was not doing anything wrong. Besides, I do not think he wanted to take me to the station house and have his nice new squad car all wet and slimy. Being a little different gets you noticed at times.

Problem Gator

I hardly ever miss a snake unless it gets down a hole, but alligators and crocodiles are different. If you catch one out of two, you are doing good. I used to catch a lot of "problem" alligators, most of them I would turn loose in a wilder area.

I got a call one day about an alligator with a dog in its mouth swimming down a canal. It was not far, so I was there in ten minutes. Sure enough, there was a nine-foot alligator with a German Shepard in its jaws and people lined up on both sides of the forty-foot wide canal.

I hooked the alligator with my heavy surf rod and 50-pound test line and a weighted treble hook on the first cast. It dropped the dog's body and took off. I held on for a minute, but it straightened out the hook. I only had one more hook since I had not planned on a gator so big. I hooked it again, but this time it went around a rock and snapped the line. You cannot catch them all, but at least they got the dog's body back.

Cold Rattlers

I had just bought a new Jeep and I was driving around trying it out and looking for new hunting areas. Just by chance, I was only a few miles from where we would buy a piece of property a few years later.

Anyway, I was driving around enjoying the new area. It was a very cool day by Florida standards. I had the heater going and I had on a heavy coat. It was probably about 50 breezy degrees, but the sun was out. I did not have much hope of finding any snakes, but I was getting stiff from riding, so I parked in an interesting looking spot.

The road cut through some pretty thick woods, almost like a tunnel without a top. The sun was high in the sky shining on the old railroad bed that ran parallel to the road. The trees blocked the wind, and it was quite pleasant.

I had not gone very far when I came to a pile of dirt and old railroad ties that had been dumped a long time ago. There lying in the sun were three big diamondback rattlers. They were in front of a hole that was under an old tie. I had a hook and a bag with me (I almost always do), so I dragged the biggest one out in the open and after a small struggle, pinned it, and put it in the bag.

I only had the one bag as I did not think there would be much out. I walked back to the car and drove up near the hole only about 50 feet away. This would save lugging them all the way back. I also had a carrying box, so I carried it to the top of the railroad bed.

The other two diamondbacks were still there, but as I lifted one up with the hook, the third one went down the hole. I dropped number two in the box and went to examine the hole. I dragged a few ties off the top of the one that the snake was under and then removed that tie. The hole was not deep and I caught number three; plus, two more. All I had to do was lift them up with the hook and set them in the box. It was pretty full. I dug around some more but did not find anything else — they were all in the one hole.

All in all, it made a very good day out of what was just a pleasure ride. Usually the best times are the unexpected ones.

Look Before You Volunteer

In Davie, Florida, there was a 50-foot-wide canal alongside of the road. I happened to look toward the canal and saw a large alligator swimming out in the middle of the canal. I had been trying to catch this gator for a few weeks but had not been able to get close to it at night when I usually go after them. This one had killed a couple of dogs and people were upset.

Apparently, this was a daytime gator and spooky at night. The gator was around eight feet long and weighed about 200 pounds. I was all alone, but what the heck, maybe I would be lucky. I had my heavy surf rig in the van, so I pulled ahead of the gator a little way, parked, and got ready. I had a big Quick Super reel with 50-pound test line and a weighted treble hook. In a few minutes, the gator came cruising along, and I dropped the hook right over it, first try. I set the hook and held on.

It was like I had hooked a car. It ran and I could not stop it for a while, but after five minutes or so it started coming in. I still did not know what I was going to do when I got it up to the bank. The road along the canal was pretty heavily traveled. A car stopped a few moments later and a guy got out. He came over to me and said, "Boy, I didn't know there was anything in this canal that big!"

I am standing there with the rod just about bent in half, sweating up a storm.

The guy says, "Do you want some help getting it in?"

"Sure," I said, "if you want."

The guy ran back to his car, opened the trunk and pulled out a landing net big enough for about a five-pound fish. I said, "I don't think that is going to be big enough."

"Sure," he says. "I have hauled in a lot of big fish with this net. I'll get its head in the net and we can flip it up on the bank."

The guy moved down near the water's edge and about then the gator broke water right near him. "Oh My God," he shouts. "I thought you had a big fish on the line. That's an ALLIGATOR!"

The rest is academic as the line broke and the gator got away. I thanked the guy for trying to help when he thought I needed it. He was still shaking when he left. A few days later, Skeet Johns and I went out in the daytime with a canoe and found the gator nearby and caught it.

That is probably why there are so many dogs in that neighborhood now.

Billboards

Now another of my favorite ways to snake hunt is checking out billboards and signs that have fallen down. They are almost as good as tin.

How many billboards the road has usually depends on the age of the road. The old main roads near the new highways are best. Because the new roads draw all the traffic, the signs are replaced, and the old signs stay up until they fall down. The most signs are on either side of the towns for a mile or two. Once you learn how to look for them, they are easy to find. You will see where the trees and bushes had been trimmed back and sometimes the posts are still there. Many of the larger billboards that are still up have been altered or fixed.

If you look around, behind or under, you may find some tin or plywood scattered about by the sign painters who did not want to haul it away. These are great finds. I have some piles of tin by billboards that are over twenty-five years old and I still catch snakes there.

I also have some that I seem to be the only person who knows where they are. There are always leaves covering it indicating no one has flipped it since the last time I was there. Remember, always put the signs, billboards, or tin back in the same place where it was. It takes a long time to get the ground beneath just the way a snake likes it unless it is in a wet spot. Billboards in wet places can be moved to dry ones.

My good buddy, Mike McDonald from Nova Scotia, thinks he knows the Latin name of just about every plant, animal and bug in America and most of the rest of the world, too. Anyway, we were out on a hunt one time up near Vero Beach, Florida on Route 1.

It was almost across from Mackee Jungle Gardens where I noticed a likely looking billboard. I parked the car and we started walking toward the sign when suddenly Mike jumped back and almost knocked me down.

"What is the matter?" I asked. I thought he had seen a rattlesnake or something.

"Only a grasshopper," he said. He is kind of jumpy at times and he can hear well. I do not hear them unless a grasshopper jumps in my ear. Jump first and ask questions later was Mike's motto.

There was a lot of tin all around the billboard, so this place looked good. Then Mike said, "I hear something hissing by the first piece of tin!"

"Well, pick it up," I said. He did and there was a four-foot indigo under it. I think was the first indigo he had caught.

We looked under several more pieces of tin panels, all about 2 feet by 20 feet, but found nothing. Then I saw a big pile of tin off to one side. It was quite wet, but I still thought something should be there. There were a lot of vines and briars all over the tin that hampered our efforts. I had to cut a lot of them away before we could lift the tin. Walking on the tin made a lot of noise and I did not have much hope of finding anything. It was very thick there, but when we got to the next to the last piece, picked it up, and there was a beautiful six-foot pine snake, one of the first ones I had ever caught. The bottom piece had water under it, so I guess the pine snake did not have any place to go.

In Texas one time, I dug through about two feet of shingles alongside of an abandoned house before I found a six-foot indigo. Never give up until you hit the bottom or water!

Another time in Georgia, I checked into a motel and wanting to stretch my legs from the long drive, I went for a walk. A block away I saw a sign lying in the bush. I lifted up the sign and there was a big five-foot canebrake rattlesnake. I hooked it into a bag and went back to the motel. I got it into my car quickly, as it was buzzing pretty good. You never know where you will find something.

Spiders, Lizards and Tree Frogs

When I used to go snake hunting from an airboat, I used to pick up a lot of miscellaneous passengers.

My air boat had a bow about four feet wide, without a sawgrass nose, so as I went through the three to six-foot tall sawgrass at 30 to 40 miles per hour. Anything hanging onto the stems would fall into the boat. The newer boats put a curved shield on the front to knock the grass down and not too much debris and critters can come into the boat.

In those days,1960's, no one wanted any of the frogs, lizards or spiders, but now they are worth catching. I can remember taking handfuls of anoles, lizards, green tree frogs, spiders, and tossing them off into the bushes.

It also got me over my dislike of spiders. Since there were so many of them, I got used to them. Sometimes after being away from the boat for an hour or so, we would come back to the boat and it looked like it was covered with a net, there were so many spider webs on it.

Good Eyes

I used to have very good eyesight before my cataracts. A lot of it was training but I'm sure I could see better than the average person. One time I was walking with a guy across a field in New York State when I happened to look in the grass and see a little red tongue flash out.

I asked the guy I was with if he could see the smooth green snake there. I pointed down by his feet and he looked but said he couldn't see it. I pointed right at it and he still couldn't see it. He got down on his knees and still couldn't find it. I told him to put his hand out, and I moved his hand until it was right over the snake before he finally saw it. True, it was only 12 inches long, but still he should have seen it.

Another time I was cruising down near Big Bend National Park in Texas and I was finding little purple worm snakes crawling on the road. Most of them were only about seven inches long, but nobody else could see them. We stopped to look at a few, only because they were something different. I was also the only one who could see the sun spiders that were on the road and on the side. I could see their eyes shine. A friend wanted a few spiders, so I caught a few, but they didn't impress me.

Another snake I learned to see was the keeled green snake. The Australian pine trees along State Road 27 sent out a lot of sucker shoots and they got pretty thick. The green snakes lay up in them at times and they blend in quite well. Their one camouflage fault is they have a bright yellow belly and if you are below them, they show up against the green.

Driving down the road, I would see three or four at a time, even doing 50 miles an hour. I would just stop where there was a bunch of them, catch the ones I could see and then drive to the next bunch. Once I caught 35 or 40 in just a few minutes. I hardly ever see any green snakes anymore. The only snakes I see many of anymore are the red rat or corn snakes. It's funny that the ones everyone wants are still common and the once common but unwanted snakes aren't common anymore.

My friend Bob Kromer, now from Gainesville, Florida, made plans to go fishing one day out in the Everglades. Yes, I do fish. I can't go snake hunting all the time. Bob brought along a friend of his named Gary. I didn't know Gary very well. We were just bank fishing for sunfish and bullheads along one of the levees that cut the Everglades up into sections. This one was about 20 feet high.

We fished for a few hours and caught a nice mess of fish. We were getting ready to head back home when Bob said, "Gary has never been out this way before. Let's show him where and how we deer hunt out here!"

I agreed, so we walked up on top of the levee where we could get a good view. The glades here were mostly sawgrass with small islands of willow trees scattered throughout. At this time of year, late summer, the water was a couple of feet deep. I was explaining how we walked and sometimes waded around, trying to chase the deer out of the willows so someone could get a shot. I happened to look out at a clump of willows about 100 yards away and saw a yellow rat snake up near the top of one of the trees.

Gary said, "No way, you couldn't see a snake that far away."

Bob said, "I see something, but I can't tell for sure." He went and got a pair of binoculars from his car, looked, and said there were two yellow snakes there.

I was half-wet anyway and it was warm, so I waded out and finally found the right tree. The under-brush was pretty thick. The tree was only as big around as my wrist. I just bent it over and picked off the yellows.

On the way back, I found another one in some ferns. I didn't have a bag with me, so I just stuffed them down in my t-shirt. Bob said he could hear me oohing and ouching for quite a ways since one would nip me now and then. Gary never doubted anything I said I saw after that.

Cottonmouths Galore

My old buddy Charlie Fitch from New York and I drove out to the Loop Road west of Miami one evening to see if we could find some snakes.

Someone had given us a tip that there were a lot of snakes out there. It was very wild in those days during the late 1950's. There were holes in the road big enough for alligators to swim in and we did see a few gators on and off the road. We took turns riding on the fender so we could catch the snakes crossing the road. Also, except for black snakes, nothing goes fast enough that you can't exit a car and catch it, but that's what we did in those days.

The canal was very low, full of hydrilla grass and between 10 and 20 feet wide. This canal was full of cottonmouths. We stopped and looked in the canal after we missed a snake, all we could see were cottonmouths. We just walked along the canal catching cottonmouths. They were all sizes, we got picky and only caught the bigger ones. We were also running out of bags to put them in.

At one place, I turned my light on and there on the other side were seven cottonmouths that I could see. I started to wade across when three of them jumped in and went under the hydrilla. I made a wide detour coming and going because I didn't catch them all and wondered where those three were. This was the most cottonmouths I had ever seen in one area. We ended up with 52 that we kept, but we probably saw 150 in three hours of hunting. We had to take them up to Ross Allen at Silver Springs in Ocala since no one in Miami could use that many. Ross Allen and Warren Prince were glad to get them.

A Snake Falls in My Hand

Here's one you will not believe. I almost don't believe it myself and I was there and had three witnesses.

I was hunting along a dirt road that was lined with Australian pine trees. They were 50 to 100 feet tall and full of corn snakes, yellow rat snakes and scarlet kings. There were two houses along the road and I often talked to the people occupying them. I had caught a few corns, and as I came to the first house, there were three people in the yard.

John was putting a new drainpipe under his driveway and he had two guys helping him. John and I used to kid around, and he was in a good mood that day. He got to telling his helpers some stories about me that really stretched the truth. They took the stories with a grain of salt since they knew John.

Then he told them how I could make snakes jump out of the trees and into my hand. They didn't buy this story. So, John told me to go stand under a particular tree and have a snake jump into my hand. I decided to humor him, so I went to the free and held out my hand. Out of the sky, a three- foot corn snake dropped right into my hand, right on cue. I tried not to act too surprised. The other guys were standing there with their mouths open, even John. They would have believed anything we told them after that.

I casually said this is a nice one, put it in a bag, and continued on my way. There just wasn't anything I could say after that. A few days later, I was back on the same road and ran into John again. He came up to me and asked, 'Frank, how did you do that?"

I just smiled and said, "It was a secret."

One thing about snake hunting is you never know what you will find next. One day, I was near Titusville looking the area over. In my travels, I came to a spot with a lot of orange groves surrounded by tall Australian pines. It was quite overgrown with lots of debris on the ground. It looked snakey to me. I hadn't gone far along these pines when I saw a nice coral snake sitting in a little patch of sun. I lifted it gently with my hook and slid it into a bag. It never knew it was caught until it was too late.

I was standing there, feeling proud of myself since I hadn't caught many corals up to that time. As I was tying the bag, I looked up into a tree and there was a four-foot corn snake about 15 feet up draped across a limb. Boy, this was great! Two snakes right together. I laid the bag with the coral snake down and climbed up the tree to catch the corn snakes.

While still elevated and tying up the bag, I looked to the ground and there was a five-foot indigo snake on the opposite side of the tree from where I had caught the coral snake. I was really excited now. It was still legal to catch indigos in those days. I came flying out of the tree and caught the indigo before it had a chance to escape. It must have been trailing the corn or the coral snake since indigos eat other snakes and it had apparently not realized I was on the other side of the tree. I didn't even have the bag tied when I saw another large coral just on the other side of a large branch, right near where the indigo had been. I got a little too excited and this coral got under a big pile of brush. I couldn't find it and I wasn't about to dig around with my hands looking for a poisonous coral snake. My hook was 30 feet away. By the time I went back and got it, the snake was gone.

I thought I had found a really great snake hunting place - well, it was for a minute, but as I continued hunting for over a half-mile, I never saw another snake. I checked the place several times after but never found another snake. I guess that's life.

Big Cottonmouth

I was snake hunting one day on the Tamiami Trail out past Forty Mile Bend. It was a nice day and I was catching a few water snakes and rat snakes. The canal there is about 30 feet wide and the space between the road and the canal is about 20 feet wide. This space is where I was concentrating my efforts.

All of a sudden, there was the biggest cottonmouth I had ever seen lying there in the tall grass. It was a little over five feet long when I measured it later. I always get excited whenever I find anything poisonous. It wouldn't still be fun if I didn't get excited. In those days I carried a hook and a bag mounted on a net frame, this was before Pillstrom tongs. It wasn't too hard to get the moccasin in the net and then into a bag.

I was feeling pretty good as I carried it back to the car. Driving ahead a short distance, I parked and started walking again. I hadn't gone very far when I looked down by my feet and there in the grass was an even bigger cottonmouth. This one was difficult. It wouldn't fit into the net and it thrashed around and struck at me like a rattlesnake. I finally managed to get it to crawl into a bag propped open on the ground.

This second cottonmouth was over six feet long. I measured it by laying it along a tile floor with one-foot square tiles and it was longer than six of them. This cottonmouth was one of the meanest snakes I had ever seen. It was all fight, I sold it to a collector who tried to claim it for a record. If it was, I didn't get credit for it. Tennant said the record is 74.5 inches. This one was bigger, and it wasn't even stretched. You can add four inches by pulling it a little. All I know is that it was the biggest one I had ever seen.

I was pretty excited as usual. As I was standing near the canal calming down, I saw a movement out of the corner of my eye. Turning around, there was an Indian with a spear raised over his head on the other side of the canal. I don't know why, but I jumped about ten feet straight up. I was pretty agile in those days. Then he started to laugh, and I laughed. He was just spearing fish.

"Boy, that was a big snake," he said. I readily agreed. I was so preoccupied that I never saw him.

It's not a good idea to take your eyes off a poisonous snake when you are trying to catch it. A friend of mine was milking a moccasin at a tourist attraction when someone asked him a question. As he looked up, the snake moved and bit him, not fatally, however.

Guard Rails and Railroad Ties

As I've said before, snakes are where you find them. Along Route 27 in Broward and Palm Beach County, there are sections of metal guardrail lying in the bushes that the road department never got around to picking up. These steel rails make great pet motels. They aren't any good on hot days, but on cool or rainy ones, they are sometimes the only places you can find anything, just like finding snakes under tin.

I'd sometimes find two or three kings or yellows or cottonmouths or whatever under one piece. Sometimes, there would only be a cotton rat or a rabbit, and I'd try to catch these to feed my snakes. I had the location of these rails memorized, so if it started to rain, I could just park by one, jump out, check it out, and then get back in without getting too wet. Those guardrails saved me from getting skunked on many rainy days.

Along the highways there isn't much for the snakes to hide under, so anything you find could have a snake in or under it. Mufflers, tires, tubes, plywood, and pieces of rug, all become hideouts. Rugs are especially good until they get wet. I found a piece of rug one day that someone had thrown out. I folded it like an accordion and set it in the bushes. A few weeks later,

I checked it and caught three nice kings in the folds. It produced snakes for over a year.

In the Carolinas, along a seldom-used rail line, we used to find kings in the rotten railroad ties. We'd cut a small stick and poke it in the holes. If a snake was home, it would exit after a few pokes. We caught quite a few that way. Another time along that same rail line, the kings weren't there, but we caught 16 cottonmouths. We finally had to quit because they got too heavy and we had to carry them over a mile back to the car. Oh, the poor lucky snake hunter.

On another rail line, I saw a tie buried in the bank and there was a hole under it. I poked my snake hook in and out came a four-foot diamondback rattlesnake. I propped open a bag so I wouldn't have to pin it and it crawled into the bag. I once again prodded the same hole and a four-foot canebrake rattlesnake came out. You don't see that very often, it was the only time for me. Talk about two species living side by side.

Fort Lauderdale Crocodile

Tommy Taylor and I both had licenses to catch nuisance alligators and we used to go out on calls quite often. Fort Lauderdale, Florida was full of alligators and people and the two were always getting in each other's way. Tommy was a professional alligator wrestler at a local tourist attraction so he could use the gators we caught in his shows. Most of the small ones we released in the Everglades.

We received a report of gators eating dogs over by a rock pit and decided to do something about it. Tommy had a nine-foot johnboat with a three-horsepower motor that was handy in the small canals. Our friend Skeet Johns was along to help. Skeet later became a professional gator wrestler and snake handler.

We put the boat in at a series of interconnected rock pits, large canals and cooling ponds, over by the Florida Power & Light plant. To catch gators in open water, I use a heavy spinning rig with 50-pound test line and a weighted treble hook. I would cast over the gator and snag it on some part of its body and then reel it in where I could get a rope on it. After that, it was just a matter of getting the gator into the boat and tying it up.

It was a calm night and we saw a couple of red eyes off in the distance. Gator eyes shine bright red in a spotlight's beam. We paddled quietly, we only used the motor for long distances, to within 50 feet of the five-foot gator. I then made a cast and hooked it. After a short fight, I brought it next to the boat where Tommy and Skeet could get a rope on it. Once in the boat, they taped the mouth shut, the most dangerous part, and tied the legs. We then went looking for another one.

In the next pit, we saw some more eyes and began paddling within casting range. This gator didn't look too big either and I dropped the hook over it on the first cast. When I set the hook, this gator about tore my arm off. I loosened the drag and held on. Boy, this one was strong!

It sure didn't look big, but it dragged us out into the middle of the pit and stopped to lie on the bottom. The water here was about 25 feet deep. I maintained steady pressure on the line and tried to pull it up and off the bottom. It would come up a little but then go down and walk along the bottom.

After a few minutes, my arms got tired so I passed the rod to Tommy for some help. Finally, after abo a half hour, the gator started to come up. We were all looking over the side of the boat when a big pointed nose instead of a round one came up.

"A croc!" we all shouted in unison. We were not expecting a crocodile and had never caught one before. Most of the crocs in Florida are found further south in the Keys and not in Fort Lauderdale. This one must have been lost or found the warm water from the plant to its liking. Recently, biologists have found more in this same place and studying them.

Regardless, we had a croc and not a gator on the line. We still had to get it into the boat and tied up. We roped its neck and paddled to shore where we could work on it more easily. We all got out and Tommy said he would get a noose around its jaws. Then we would able to handle it more safely. After all, we are a little crazy but not stupid.

Skeet was on one side with the rope and I was on the other side with the rod. Tommy leaned out to put the noose around the croc's jaws and the croc lunged at him. Its jaws snapped about a foot from Tommy's face and the croc dropped into the water at Tommy's feet. Skeet and I had to steady Tommy until he got his composure back.

After all of us were calm, we got the croc tied up and loaded. When measured later, the croc was 8 feet 3 inches and weighed 200 pounds. We must have been quite a sight coming back what with croc's head tied to the bow and its tail on the back seat. Skeet and I stood on either side of the croc with the smaller gator under our legs. The boat was only three inches above the water and we had to go a mile. Luckily, the croc never made a move of any kind. We were all happy for this since we had had enough excitement for one night.

There was even a story and our picture in the Miami Herald something about the first crocodile caught in that area in years.

Tommy Taylor & Frank Weed moving a crocodile from one enclosure to another

Monkey Business

Sometimes things work out better than I planned. Like the time one of my neighbors phoned and said there was a chimpanzee running around outside her home. I was the designated neighborhood catcher of beasties, opossums in the pool or garage, snakes and alligators were just about everywhere.

Living in the country, there was always some animal in the wrong place. When it was a snake, it was always eight feet long. When you got to where the snake was, you were lucky if it was a three-footer. Consequently, I wasn't really expecting much. The only vehicle available at my house was a pickup with a camper on it. I grabbed a pole net and one of those plastic airline crates and drove to the neighbor's house.

As I pulled into the yard, I saw a pretty big chimpanzee come around the house. It was about 40 pounds and much too big and strong to fit in the net or the crate. I sat there for a moment studying the chimp. I thought it seemed pretty friendly. Then I noticed a bag of oranges that I had picked earlier. I took a few oranges and went around to the back of the truck and opened the camper door. The chimp came over, I showed it the oranges and threw a couple inside. The chimp went right in and I shut the door, the easiest catch I have ever made.

Now, I had the chimp but what was I going to do with it? I called the dog pound, but they had no reports of missing chimps. Since all of this had started in the late afternoon, it was now dark. I decided to go snake hunting out in front of this house for a few minutes along the road. I had barely started when I noticed some people coming my way with flashlights. I didn't think they were snake hunting.

When they approached, I asked them, "Are you looking for a chimp?"

They said, "Yes, how did you know?" I took them over to the camper and told one of the guys to open the door. He did so and out jumped the chimp into his arms.

It seemed they were visiting another neighbor of mine and had decided to go into town. Upon returning, they realized their chimp had escaped from its temporary quarters in the neighbor's dog kennel even though it was locked. They had been looking for it for a while, and I saved them some time and trouble. I didn't even take the reward they offered. It's not every day I get to catch a chimpanzee.

Crocs in the Mangroves

Dad and I were in Jamaica catching crocodiles. One night we were trying a new place, I think it was called the Milk River. We went down near the mouth where it emptied into a bay. We had gone up river the night before and had done quite well. On this night, we were just looking the place over to see what was there. The closer we got to the salt water the more mangrove trees there were, and they got bigger too.

The mangrove tree looks like it is standing on tiptoes, many of the roots are up in the air but there are also roots in the muck. It looks like a spider with fifty legs standing in shallow water. These roots are so close together you cannot walk through them. A snake would have difficulty crawling through them. I'm sure you get the picture.

As we paddled around, we found small crocs out in the open part of the river proper and we were catching a few. However, we were seeing many crocs back under the mangrove roots where we couldn't cast over them. In open water, you can cast a treble hook beyond the croc and reel it in until snagging the croc. Then the tussle begins until the croc is boat side. We were only after small ones this trip and I wanted to figure out how to reach the small ones under the roots.

Suddenly, it came to me. I told Dad to paddle straight toward one under the roots. When we got in as far as the roots would allow, I took the rod, pushed it slowly toward the croc, dropped the hook behind it, and then hooked it. The hooked croc would dive down and swim for the main river. We then backed up a little and reached down into the water with the paddle until we snagged the line. We then just hand-over-handed the line until we got to the croc. Most of them were two footers. After we got the croc in a box, I'd cut the hook loose and reel in the line.

A few would pull the hook loose going through the roots, but we caught many we wouldn't have caught any other way. A croc has got to get up pretty early in the morning to fool me.

Jamaica Wreck

I went with Ross Kananga one day to help with one of his crocodile wrestling shows out towards Ocho Rios, Jamaica. This is where I saw the bats coming out of the woods and where I went the next night to catch the boas. On the way back, we came upon an accident. The narrow road had been cut through a hill with about ten-foot sides and a mini-bus had collided with a police car. The bus ended up lying on its side totally across the road. We could not get by.

We got out to see what we could do to help. There was a group of people standing around, but no one seemed to be doing anything. One woman was acting crazy, dancing around and making noises. We finally found out that there was a dead girl in the bus, killed in the crash, and the crazy woman was the girl's mother. Someone explained she was doing some sort of death ritual. Weird!

Several of the passengers were injured but were walking around. There were no other vehicles around as it was one in the morning. We said we would take the people to the hospital, but we had to turn the bus so we could get by. The people there said they could not touch the bus with the dead girl in it. Ross and I crawled in and carried the dead girl out.

We laid her by the side of the road and covered her with a couple of bags. Then we all got together and swung the bus around. Now at least, we could get by.

Ross, Jim Gore, Elizabeth (Ross's lady friend), and I were in the front seat of Jim's pick-up. Our two helpers plus seven of the injured were in the back. We just started to leave when one of the police officers who was in the wreck showed up. He had gone for help. We told him we were taking the people to the hospital. He said something to Ross that I could not understand. I have trouble with the dialect.

Ross got all upset and said, "No, no, drive on, Jim!" and away we went.

I asked Ross what the constable had said. He said that he knew we had a full load, but could we tie the girl's body on to the front fender? We would have been quite a sight driving through town with a dead girl's body tied to the fender. I used to feel bad having a dead deer tied to the car up north, but this was something else.

We got them all to the hospital okay with no more troubles. by the way, I almost forgot to mention, there were two seven-foot crocodiles in the back of the truck that I don't think anyone noticed.

Gators for a Croc

My father and I went down to Jamaica a couple of times catching crocodiles. We mostly caught the smaller ones because they were easier to transport. You could carry 20 or so home in a small cardboard box right on the plane with you.

On the first trip, the only boats we could find to borrow or rent were big heavy wooden ones. The next time we went, we shipped down a 12-foot aluminum johnboat. With a three hp motor, it could go anywhere. We stayed with a friend of ours, Jim Gore, a crocodile hunter from way back. He used to take Errol Flynn, the actor, out shooting and catching crocs.

We went out a few nights and caught a bunch of small crocs. As we were getting ready to return home to Florida, Jim said he liked the light boat and wondered if we would sell it. He said he didn't have much money, but he'd trade one of his crocs for it. He had a backyard full of them, most of them in a small pond surrounded by junked cars.

Crocs were everywhere, we even had to chase one out from under the kitchen table that was after a cat before we could eat breakfast. We knew a guy that wanted a larger croc, so we made a deal. I caught a nice seven-footer out of the pond, and we loaded it into a crate.

Returning to Florida, we took the croc up to a guy who had a small alligator farm. Now he didn't have much money at the time either, so we ended up with 28 baby alligators. Since these gators came from a licensed dealer, we could sell them legally. They were funny little guys who would eat out of my hand. Whenever I cleaned their pool, they'd all get in and fight with the broom, making it hard to clean. I'd talk to them (gator talk) and most of them would start to bellow. It was funny to see two foot gators bellowing. I didn't really think they did that until they were bigger. We sold most of them and we released the last few into a pond at our new place in Immokalee, Florida.

Fresh Water Shrimp

Dad and I were out catching crocodiles one night in Jamaica. We were paddling up a very pretty little river that we had never been on before. It was only about 25 feet wide, six to eight feet deep and crystal clear with a slow current.

We were catching a few small crocs mostly by hand. We did not want any big ones this time. I had a few fishing poles with treble hooks, but we did not need them here. It was easier to just grab them. We also had a frog gig with us that the guy we were staying with said we would need. Jim Gore was an old crocodile hunter who used to take Errol Flynn out croc hunting when he was in Jamaica making those pirate movies.

I was out with Jim one night, each of us was in his own boat, when Jim saw a croc out in the bay. He had his man row over to it. Jim stood in the bow with a spear on a beautiful moonlit night, and he reminded me of Captain Ahab going after Moby Dick. He stuck it in the tail with the spear and it made a pretty bad wound. I never really liked spears after that, but we had the little spear just in case.

Returning to the river, I happened to shine the light down into the water and I saw all these little red eyes shining all along the bottom. Looking closer, I saw they were fresh water shrimp. Some were really big ones, over a foot long, two feet long with their legs stretched out.

We decided to take a little time and catch a little snack. So, I got out the spear and in just a few minutes, we had all we wanted, half a cooler full. They were a very pretty blue and green. The ones in Florida are dark brown and not as big. The tails on these were as big as chicken drumsticks.

We continued on. catching a few more crocs and a few big shrimp we just could not pass up. All of a sudden, the river stopped and went straight down. It was a spring. It was beautiful looking down into that clear water with sides covered with all these red glowing shrimp eyes.

We tried to buy or lease the area with Ross Allen for a crocodile and shrimp farm, but we could not make a deal with the Jamaican Government. It would have been an awesome place. I could have stayed there forever!

We took the cooler full back to Jim's place. Pearl, Jim's cook, did a wonderful job on them. The only thing wrong was I wish I had gotten more because they were so good!

A Croc Scare

Another time Dad and I were down in Jamaica chasing a few crocodiles around. We had the 12- foot johnboat and were paddling the Milk River. This area was mostly sugar cane and, in places, it grew right down to the river. A lot of the cane hung over the water and it was as thick as the mangroves further down the river.

As we paddled along, I saw a bunch of red eyes shining back in the sugar cane. There must have been two dozen baby crocs back there. I kind of leaned over the front of the square-nosed boat as Dad paddled ahead. I was grabbing the babies left and right and handing them back to Dad who was putting them in bags. They were making quite a racket with all their grunts. We had just back paddled out a little to get a better angle when this big eight-foot croc popped up right next to us. It was probably the mother.

It roared almost like a lion, I never heard one roar like that before or since, and it came right for the boat. I pulled back into the boat in record time, but it was all a bluff as Mama Croc went right under the boat and disappeared. I grabbed the heavy rod to snag it, but it didn't show itself again. I was just as glad because my nerves were a little bent!

Airport Crocodiles

Skeet Johns and I took a trip to Jamaica to hunt crocodiles for a change of pace. I didn't know about the Jamaican boas yet, but I had caught a few crocs before with my dad. We hunted mostly around Kingston and the Milk River on the south coast since there weren't any crocs on the north coast.

After three nights, we had about 40 small crocs, babies up to three feet. The small ones are a lot easier to catch, handle, and carry. We caught a few bigger ones for the fun of it but gave them to the guy we were staying with who had a bunch in his backyard that he liked to play with. When it was time to leave, we packed them in cardboard boxes.

The bigger ones had their jaws taped shut and some tape on their legs. The babies were bagged and put in a cardboard box. We went to the airport and checked them in as baggage, things were easier in those days. It was raining quite a bit that day and I was looking out of the window at them loading the plane. I knew they did not have a cover over the bags on the luggage cart, but I did not think anything about it at the time. We boarded the plane and were back in Miami in less than an hour. I think the fare was forty dollars round trip. We left the plane and went down to the baggage claim.

We finally found the right place, moved up to the carousel and conveyor. Just then a couple of people in front of me jumped back and almost knocked me down. I looked at the carousel and there was a wet cardboard box with a three-foot croc halfway out. The rain had turned the cardboard to mush. I quickly put my jacket over the box and got it out of the way before too many people saw it. We went back a little later and got the rest of our stuff with no damage done.

Jamaican Boas

"Hey Frank, come on down to Jamaica and catch me some boas. I'll pay your way."

I left the next day to see what I could do for Ross Kananga. Ross and I had worked together for three months for a rodeo in South America. He had a crocodile farm and tourist attraction near Montego Bay. Ross was quite busy doing shows, wrestling crocodiles at different hotels and resorts. He asked a friend to drive me out to the country where it was said to be crawling with snakes. We have all heard that before, sometimes it was true, sometimes not.

We trudged all over the woods that night where every bush and tree brandished huge thorns. The only thing we saw were land crabs. Finally, instead of fighting our way back through all those thorns, I suggested we walk back on the road. This made the trip back longer, but both of us would save a lot of blood. Upon reaching the road, I told my companion that in Florida I hunted snakes by shining my headlamp on the bushes along the road. With that said, the first bush contained a beautiful seven-foot boa. So much for fighting thorns anymore.

The next day, Ross was doing a show in Ocho Rios and I went along to help. We went to the show just before darkness fell. I noticed bats flying in the woods and across the road. Ross said there were some cliffs along the north coast, and I figured that's where the bats were during daylight. I also knew that boas ate bats, so I noted a few places where I saw the most bats.

The next evening, a friend of Ross's, Brenda Barnes, agreed to drive me around. I did not like driving on the wrong side of the road. In truth, it was bad enough just riding on the wrong side as a passenger. Brenda owned the Banana Boat Club in Montego Bay, and Ross and I hung out there on the few nights I didn't go hunting.

We went to where I had seen the bats the night before. I gave Brenda a flashlight hoping she would help. About 30 feet into the woods, I saw a small cave in a cliff with lots of bats flying around. At the opening was a large rock straddled by a boa trying to catch bats as they flew by. I guess the boa had not figured out how to get into the cave yet.

With Brenda's help, I caught two more in the next hour. They were easy to find once you knew where to look. I also caught five of the miniature boas under rocks. They only get about two feet long and look like garter snakes. They were cute and probably rarer than the big ones.

Brenda had to get back to the club, so we called an end to snake hunting for the night. We then closed the club at 3 a.m., it had been a long day.

A few months later, I returned to Jamaica for a vacation with Pauline Gammon, my girlfriend at the time. We were at Ross's when Brenda showed up. We had a nice visit, but later Pauline said that even though I had told her that I had been hunting with Brenda, I didn't tell her that she looked like THAT! Well, she was pretty cute. The next couple of nights were the coldest I ever spent in Jamaica.

Another time when Ross and I were doing some hunting, I noticed a little patch of snakeskin in a limestone ledge. There was a snake in a hole that was too small for me to get my fingers into. I tried poking it out with a stick without success. Finally, Ross came over and drew his .357 mag revolver and fired two shots right beside the hole. The rock crumbled, and I was now able to extricate the snake unharmed. Ross was a little impatient at times.

It was always fun when someone like Ross paid me to travel.

Just Another Jamaican Croc

Jamaica became a favorite destination for croc hunting whenever Dad and I needed a little excitement, or in this case, some excitement for a few Florida friends. We were using our 12-foot johnboat and were on the Milk River. We had caught a few smallish crocs and were having a good time. Nothing really exciting had happened yet.

As we proceeded further up the river, it got pretty shallow. The river was about 20 feet wide but only a foot deep and the bottom was obscured by the thick grass growing there. Suddenly, there was a commotion under the boat because we had poled on top of an eight- foot croc. The croc went crazy!

It came out from under the boat, hit the bank, and came back under the boat. It then went out the other side, hit the other bank, and ended up under the boat again. By this time, all four of us were standing and trying to figure out what to do. Every time we started to vacate the boat, the croc would come back, so we just stayed put and held our breath. Finally, the croc figured out where it was, swam downstream, and disappeared. It was an exciting few minutes, but we were glad to see it go in spite of not catching it. Our friends always looked to Dad and me to put a little extra excitement into their lives.

A Long, Long Ride

Years ago, Joe, a neighbor of mine, was moving to Nicaragua in Central America. He asked me to help drive and to keep him company. He would pay our way down and fly me back.

"How soon do you want me ready?" I asked. A few days later, after some injections and visas, off we went. He, me, and a German Shepard named Kellogg traveled south in a pickup with a camper.

Our ride through the southwestern states was uneventful and in three days we arrived at the Mexican border. The customs guys looked at our papers and then wanted the back of the truck opened. When I did, Kellogg growled, the inspector said, "Go on, adios, enjoy your trip to Mexico."

We didn't see any snakes in Mexico since it was very hot, 100 degrees or more at times. Driving after dark was dangerous because Mexico didn't require fences for livestock, and they all ran loose. We stuck to the main roads such as they were. Parts of the Pan American Highway were still gravel.

One day, some guy passed us doing 100 miles an hour and plowed right through a flock of sheep killing about ten of them. We kept looking for whoever was chasing him, but no one came. He must have been really late for a date!

We helped the little kid, who was watching the sheep, drag the bodies off the road. The boy was very upset, so we gave him five dollars which cheered him up a little.

One of the strangest things I saw down there was a young boy peddling a bicycle out in the middle of the bush. On the bike he had two 10-pound pigs tied on either side of the back wheel and about 10 chickens hanging from the handlebars. All the animals were hanging upside down and we couldn't imagine where the boy was going.

Another thing I remember happened at a restaurant one morning. The waitresses had on long gowns that touched the floor. When they walked, it looked like they were skating. They just seemed to float across the floor, it was quite enchanting.

Just outside of Guatemala City, there was a roadblock on the highway. A police officer said he would guide us around the city. We asked what was going on and he said there was a little shooting, just a small revolution. We got around okay, hearing only a few shots.

However, before we got back to the main road, we came upon two young Indian boys walking along. They each had a large machete on their belts. The cop said something we didn't quite catch. We thought he wanted us to stop and pick them up, but as we slowed down, the cop got all excited and drew his gun.

"Go, go, go!" he said. We got past them, and the cop said they were "malo" (bad). The cop related how they had to lock themselves in the jail at night or they would be killed. Sounds like a great place to live. We dropped the cop off on the other side of town and resumed our journey.

We drove for many miles but then came to another roadblock. This time the road was blocked by a landslide, but we could take the old road. I have been on better cow paths. We went up a steep winding road in first gear and down in first. All these delays slowed us down so that darkness caught us before getting to the next town.

There was hardly any traffic and, when rounding a corner, there was an Indian lying in the road. The police had told us not to stop for anyone because bandits would come out of the bushes and rob us. We went around him but felt badly. However, it was better than being robbed. We called the police from the hotel and reported it, but I doubt if anyone checked on that Indian.

We finally arrived in Managua, Nicaragua after eight or nine days. Joe rented a house since he was planning on bringing his family down. His wife was originally from this area. The next day I went exploring a little, I was tired of riding. I looked in a lot of thick trees but found nothing. In fact, I never saw a snake down there.

The next day, we went to Granada which is on Lake Nicaragua. This lake is famous for its fresh-water sharks. I didn't see any, but I didn't see anyone swimming either. We hired a boat big enough to hold 20 people and rode around the lake for a couple of hours.

The cost was a grand total of six dollars. All I saw was a bunch of large turtles with slate-black shells.

The next day, Joe had to go to town, and I walked off in a different direction to see what I could find. I found a big hole about 200 yards across and 50 feet deep. In the bottom were bushes and water. It was the only water I had seen, and I thought there just might be something there.

Without thinking, I do that a lot, I jumped into the hole and slid halfway to the bottom. It was a cinder crater left over from the many volcanoes in this area. My intention was to look at the swampy end of the hole, but I got a bad feeling.

The sides of this crater were all cinders, the lava rocks you use in gas grills. I would take two steps up and slide back three. I was getting nowhere fast but it was hot, it was over 100 degrees. I finally managed to crawl and wiggle up enough to grab a few roots and get out. I can tell you, I was worried for a while. I felt like an ant in a lion's hole. This place bothered me. I get premonitions now and then, and I had several there.

There were two volcanoes erupting a little in the area, one to the north and one to the south. I thought I could feel one coning up right under me. A year later, there was a bad earthquake that killed many people.

I had another premonition a few days later, but I will mention it now. When my plane took off from the airport, I saw out the window that there was a shantytown at the end of the runway. I could imagine a plane not getting off the ground and demolishing those shacks. Guess what? That's exactly what happened less than a year later killing 80 on the plane and 80 on the ground.

After getting out of the hole, I walked near a cow pasture and among the cows were spiny-tailed iguanas, two to three feet long. I decided to see if I could catch one; however, as soon as I got close, they all climbed up trees. Since I could climb pretty good, I figured I could still catch them. Halfway up the tree, however, they all jumped out and climbed another tree. This tactic continued for quite a while. If I had some friends with nets, it would have been easy to catch them. I was able to catch ten of these nice lizards anyway.

A friend of Joe's had a farm way out in the woods and wanted Joe to take a look at it. With a little time to spare, Joe agreed. There were four guys who needed a ride to the same place, and we took them with us, mostly to show us the way. The road was only a trail and even calling it a trail was an understatement. It was a logging road, but the last trucks out had left deep ruts in the mud which had hardened.

They were so deep, we had to straddle them in places. It was only 35 miles to the farm, but it felt like a hundred. The ride was interesting, but the forest grew right to the edge of the road making it dark. We did see lizards crossing the trail and caimans in the streams, so I thought I might hunt for them after we got there.

There were four of us in the front seat and two guys in the back with the dog. In the middle of the night, Joe wanted to stop and rest a little. One of our group knew a place where we could get some coffee. We stopped at a lean-to covered with banana leaves and mud. There was a couple sleeping in hammocks and they got up when we pulled In.

On a makeshift stove, there was a big iron kettle. The woman poured some water from a five-gallon can into the kettle and threw in a handful of coffee beans. This was added to the old coffee already in the kettle. In a few minutes, she dipped some tin cans into the brew and gave us each one. I was so tired and beat up that I would have drunk anything. I regretted this. About a half hour later it all came up, and what didn't come up came out the lower end. Ever since then I have a hard time even smelling coffee.

At daylight, we came to the last hill before the village. There was a brook at the bottom of the hill and we couldn't get enough speed to get across the brook and up the other side. We did get halfway up and then had to unload the truck. Joe backed down and across the brook. Then he gunned the truck. Upon reaching us, we jumped behind and pushed him up over the top. Now we had to reload everything.

The village was about 25 thatched roof huts surrounded by fields. I still wasn't feeling well from the previous night's coffee, so the group let me rest on a cot in one of the huts. After an hour, a noise woke me up. There was a large pig eating bananas next to my cot. I chased it out and blocked the door. I did finally start to feel better, so I decided to take a walk.

There were cows, pigs, and chickens all running loose everywhere. At the end of a dirt street, I saw some water. A woman was coming toward me from that direction with a five-gallon can on her head. She stopped and said something I could not understand. Then she set the can down and dipped out a glassful and handed it to me. It was green and I thought it was lime Kool-Aid. However, since my stomach was still so upset, I declined it with the little Spanish I knew. I continued toward the water.

The water was actually a river pool because it was the dry season. The pool was green. It was as green as what I thought was the lime Kool-Aid. The cows and pigs were wading in it as well as people were washing themselves and their clothes in it. Kids were swimming in it and the village sewerage was running into it. This was their drinking water?

Thank goodness we had some Pepsi colas along or I probably wouldn't be alive today. Joe talked to some of the people and one couple said that they had had eight kids but only three lived, the toughest ones. The place was so unhealthy looking that two of the guys that had come with us to work there begged us to take them back. We did.

They thought if they stayed, they would die there. Joe used my feeling bad as an excuse to get us out of there. Besides, I didn't see any sign of snakes. The return ride was equally rough and I was starting to look forward to the good old USA.

Flying back to Miami, I was a little worried about my box of lizards. I had no papers for them, but the customs inspector just asked me if I had any Mary Jane.

I said, "Who?"

He said, "If you don't know who, then you don't have any."

I did not have any marijuana, only lizards, and I was home free.

Tarantulas

Living in southeast Florida, you get used to the land crabs walking across roads. The first time I was out in Texas, Charlie Fitch and I were inland and saw a small land crab in the middle of the road. We didn't pay any attention to it until it hit both of us at the same time, there aren't any land crabs in the desert. It must have been a tarantula. We made a quick U-tum and it was still there. The only thing we could put it in was a coffee can, which we did. A few miles further, we found another one and put it in the same can. Upon finding a third one, we saw only one tarantula in the can with a few legs. One had eaten the other. We learned what not to do in a hurry!

Several years later, Jimmy Wass and I were night road hunting. We were catching a few snakes, but in a one half-mile stretch of highway we found a bunch of squashed tarantulas and a few live ones. All of them were males, black and long-legged. We returned to this same place in daylight to investigate. The road cut through a couple of hills with sloping banks about 30 feet high. These banks were full of spider holes.

The holes were six to ten inches deep. With light, we could see a spider in almost every hole. I had a small folding shovel, but it didn't work in the rocky soil. We also didn't think the Texas Road Department would like us digging up the side of the highway. We finally figured an easy way to get them out. I took a black-eyed susan, a flower with a long stem, and stuck it down the hole.

Sometimes the spider grabbed it thinking it was food, and you could pull the spider out. If that didn't work, you could push the flower past and under the spider and then lift up and goose the spider out.

I had a bunch of Dixie paper cups and lids just in case I found some spiders. I knew from the past to keep each tarantula separated. It was simple to place the cup over the spider, slip the lid under, flip the cup, and seat the lid. We punched a few holes in the top and we were ready for more. We caught 100 spiders in two hours and they were all nice big females, brown and fat. We filled a couple of cardboard boxes with the cups and continued scouting.

Sometimes we camped out in the woods or in the desert or wherever we were. It started to rain that night, so we had to sleep in the van. We spread our sleeping bags on top of wooden boxes occupied by 25 rattlers. Every time we rolled over, they would start rattling, it was a nice lullaby. Everything was fine until dawn when a tarantula walked over my face. I woke up in a hurry, turned on a light, and there were spiders everywhere. They had easily chewed through the paper cups.

In the next town, we bought some plastic cups and solved the problem. However, we found spiders crawling in the van for the next week.

Goins King

On the way to Texas to catch snakes one time, I was in north Florida in an area where the blotched king snake aka goins is found. I always like to catch something new, so I drove around awhile until I found a place that looked right. I had no idea what type area they liked but this particular spot looked good to me.

I had only walked a few minutes when I saw a stump. Stumps are good in the Carolinas for kings and I figured they were good for kings in Florida too. So, I walked over and there was a four-foot king stretched out alongside the stump. Sometimes my luck scares me. I picked it up, put it in a bag, and continued on my way to Texas happy to add another subspecies to my list.

On the way back from Texas a few weeks later, I stopped right along the main road, State Road 90. This was before the I-10 days. I had a lot of snakes in the car and could not leave them in the sun long, but my legs had gotten stiff and I needed a walk. I had not taken ten steps when there was another Goins king. These are the only two I have ever caught.

Also, that same day I remembered I had a yellow rat snake that had a bad scar making it un-saleable. I kept forgetting to turn it loose. So, the next time I got stiff from so much driving, I stopped right along the road in a nice wooded area. I walked into the woods a little way and set the yellow loose. It crawled a few feet away and right over a nice gulf hammock rat snake that I had not noticed. I think that was a very good trade. It was the only rat snake of that subspecies I ever caught.

A Texas Ranch Hunt

A friend and fellow snaker, Jimmy Wasserman from Houston, called me at my grandmother's house in Houston where I was staying and asked if I wanted to go out to his uncle's ranch to do some snake hunting. For me, that's a silly question.

His uncle had called, said he was seeing a lot of snakes lately, and wanted Jimmy to catch them because he did not like them. Jimmy likes to hunt almost as much as I do, so away we went. We hunted often together when I was in Texas.

The ranch was about 100 miles from Houston. Jimmy had not been there lately and was not too familiar with the area. When we finally found it, we visited with his relatives for a few minutes and then off we went.

Out behind the barn, we found a pile of fence posts and railroad ties that looked like a good place to start. With one of us at each end of a post, we started moving the pile. It was not that big. By the time we got to the bottom of the pile we had three Texas rat snakes, a pretty good start.

We then moved out through the fields where there was a lot of cactus, mesquite, and brush— good looking snake country. We walked and walked but we were not finding anything. It was a nice day, not too hot or sunny, and it seemed just right to me.

We wandered around a while looking under the trees where it looked so good but found nothing. We decided to go back to the house for some lunch and try a different area later. We cut across an open field that we had been avoiding and headed towards the house.

Somewhere towards the middle, there were some short bushes that had sprouted up from where they had cut the trees down to clear the area. The armadillos had dug little short holes under these bushes. I happened to look in one of these holes and there was a coiled western diamondback. We caught it and started looking in more holes and almost everyone had a snake in it. It was a dumb place to be, but there they were. We were late for lunch, but we did not mind since we had caught 12 rattlers.

After a short rest, we went to another section of the ranch that his uncle recommended. We wandered around and caught a few more rattlers. When all of a sudden, I had a feeling.

I started to say to Jimmy, "We haven't caught a bull snake" but before I could finish there was a nice big bull snake in a clump of cactus. Tongs are really handy in cactus. I tonged it out, all six feet of it.

A little farther on, I was poking in another clump of cactus, when another bull snake rattled, blew air. It sounds just like a rattlesnake and really makes you jump until you get used to it. You should still jump just in case it is a rattlesnake.

We caught a few more bulls and rattlers before we had to leave as Jimmy had something important to do back in Houston. It was a very good hunt just the same. I do not let many important things get in the way of my snake hunting.

Frank and friends

Lizards

Driving around out in west Texas one pleasant day, I came to an area where numerous flat rocks were scattered around in the fields. This looked interesting and I like tuning over rocks. You never know what you are going to find under a rock.

Most of the rocks were not too big, two to three feet, good turning sizes. I turned one rock and there was a collared lizard under it. It took off like a shot and went under another rock ten feet away. I went over to the second rock, turned it over, and the lizard went back to the first rock.

In poisonous snake country, it is not a good idea to pick something up and just grab. There may be a poisonous snake under there, too.

Now, I know there wasn't anything else under that first rock except the lizard. I got ready, turned over the rock, grabbed and caught it. I caught several more lizards using this same technique. I also did find a few rattlers, garters and a small bull snake.

A day or so later at a lower elevation, I started finding banded geckos under things. They are easy to catch since they do not run. You have to be careful that you do not hurt them, though, as they are very delicate.

They did not impress me much at the time. Thirty years ago I liked bigger game. Now they are quite valuable and in demand, but in those days, I caught what I found. I was not looking for lizards, but if I found one, I tried to catch it as everything had some value. One lizard equaled one gallon of gas, one snake was a motel for a night, etc.

Two Quick Westerns

I was out riding the roads one night in west Texas with my eleven-year old nephew, Kurt MacLaughlin. We were catching a few odd snakes, kings, a nice bull snake and a couple of hognose snakes.

Then I saw a big western diamondback just barely on the pavement. The grass on the shoulder was pretty high. I approached and stopped about 20 feet from the rattler and kept the headlights on it.

Kurt was excited about catching a rattler and this was the first one we had seen. I did not want it to get in the tall grass, so I gave Kurt the tongs and told him to drag it to the middle of the road where we could handle it more safely.

Luckily, we were the only car on the road. The tongs were four feet long, so he was perfectly safe even though the snake was a little over five feet long. I grabbed for a lock box from the back of the Jeep.

Just as I got the box out, Kurt started hollering, "Uncle Frank, there's another one coming out on the road."

Sure enough, there was another big rattler crawling out of the grass. They must have been getting ready to mate and the second one came out to see what the first one was doing in the middle of the road.

Well, I set the box down by the first one and opened the lid. Kurt had all he could do to get it in the box because the snake was longer than he was tall. He said I had better catch the second rattler because he was tired. I took the tongs, picked up the snake, put it in the box, closed the lid, and put the box back in the Jeep. Two quick rattlesnakes!

Worm Snakes

I was recently digging in my compost pile for fishing worms when I turned over a big clod of dirt and out came a rather large worm. It acted a little differently than a normal worm. I picked it up to see it was not slimy.

Looking closer, I could see it had scales and a tongue. I had never seen one like it before. I looked it up in a book and it was a Brahminy Blind Snake from Asia that has become naturalized in Florida. It wasn't much but it was something new to me.

Years ago, I was hunting down by Big Bend National Park in Texas. I was road hunting with a few friends one night, just cruising around since we did not know the area. Normally when you hunt at night, you look out as far as your car lights reach. Anything large you can easily see in the distance but for the small stuff, you have to be closer.

I think I have good eyesight and thought I was seeing very small worms or something on the road. The road was macadam aka gravel over tar and these things were crawling around in the gravel, quite hard to see. When the better snakes stopped crawling, I finally stopped to look at one of the worms. No one else had seen them. It was a worm snake, not more than six inches long. They were a pretty lavender on top and pink on the belly. I drove around and found a few more to look at later. The next day we looked them over and then turned them loose. We didn't see any value in them. They were not much but another snake to add to our life list of snakes found.

Driving around the back roads north of Houston, I came upon a dead snake on the road that I couldn't identify at first. It was kind of bluish with white spots all over it and about four feet long. I finally identified it in a snake book as a buttermilk racer. Never having caught one, I decided to hunt one up. I knew they were in that area, so I found a likely looking spot and started walking.

The country there was heavily wooded, but with clearings here and there, plus, a few little brooks running through them. It was a real pretty place and if I were a snake, I would like it there.

Walking up to a blown down magnolia tree, I saw two copperheads lying by the roots. I propped open a bag on a bush, lifted them up one at a time with my hook and put them in the bag. A few steps farther, there were two more. I caught these and 50 feet farther there were two more. My bag was beginning to get full. I came to a patch of woods that was so thick the sun didn't shine through except for one little shaft of light. The light was shining on what I thought was a white rock, but when I went over, it was a bleached cow skull and right on top of it was a pigmy rattlesnake. It was just like someone had set it up for me. It was the only pigmy rattlesnake I ever caught out west.

I finally found two buttermilks coiled on a bush, I could only catch one, they were fast. I did catch two more buttermilks and a couple more copperheads on the way back to the car.

I thought I did really good for the first time in strange country. It looked so much like the woods in Connecticut, I felt right at home.

Mexican Milksnakes

I decided to take a trip to Texas in the late 1960's so I could catch something different. I knew where and how to hunt in Florida, but I did not know Texas yet. I was hoping to get lucky. I would mostly be road hunting at night, but on the cooler days I could walk around and hunt. Finding a dead snake on a road was a good sign that there were more snakes in that area.

However, some of this country had so little traffic that there aren't any snakes run over. Also, the buzzards, hawks, crows and ants clean up the snakes quickly eliminating the evidence.

There was one road I almost didn't go back to because I hadn't seen anything dead on that road in the daytime. At night, this same road was crawling with snakes.

I found a five-mile stretch of road near Laredo where I could catch two or three snakes on every pass. They were nothing fancy, just kings, hognose or rattlesnakes. My real goal was a Mexican milksnake since I had never caught one and it had the most value.

After five passes without meeting another car, I saw a car coming at me. I thought to myself, "He will probably run over something good."

Low and behold, there was a Mexican milk writhing on the road after he passed my car. That spoiled my whole evening. It's a shame to find a $50 snake dead on the road after coming so far to find one.

A few days later, I found another dead milksnake on a side road and decided to try it that night. I had three friends including Jimmy Wasserman with me this time. We had just started road cruising when we met a few cars coming at us. We found out later that there was an oil well out there and this was a shift changing. Within a mile of the passing cars, we found a dead milk and then two more. The toll finally ended with seven dead milks. We were all sick. Then we saw another one. I stopped to take a look, and it started to crawl away.

"It's alive!" I shouted. It looked like a Chinese fire drill as four people tried to exit two doors. In this madness, I had to jump back into the car and set the brake. I still managed to catch the snake. We caught one more down the road. At least nine milks had crawled up that ten-mile stretch of road that night. We hunted it again a couple of nights later and never saw another snake. It was the same time and weather. Just when you think you have it all figured out, you realize you don't.

I drove 11,000 miles in seven weeks and learned a great deal. It's a good thing gas was 23 cents a gallon then and catching a few good snakes could pay your way.

The Joy of Road Hunting

In different parts of the country about the only and most effective way to find snakes and a few other things is to ride the roads. Generally, I drive in the late afternoon, evening and night. Mornings are good also for the daytime crawlers until it gets too hot.

The temperature is the main thing, too hot or too cold and they do not crawl. In Texas, I would get a motel room, drive around four or five hours at dark, go back to the motel, and sleep until daylight. Then I drove around until 10 a.m., went back to the motel, ate, and slept until dusk again. After doing this for about three days, I would wake up at 7 a.m. and I couldn't remember if it was a.m. or p.m. I would then do something else for a few days.

I remember one night I was very groggy from lack of sleep and I stopped to look in one of those cattle guards, a three-foot-deep cement trough with steel bars on top across a driveway to keep the cattle from walking out. A lot of critters fall into these troughs and cannot get out. The snakes go in and eat them and some of the snakes cannot get out either.

Anyway, I looked into this one, and there was a coral snake. I had a pair of barbeque tongs just for these small poisonous snakes, so I scooped it up, dropped it in a bag, and called it a night. The next day I finally got around to checking the coral snake and it was a very dark Mexican milksnake, ten times more valuable than a coral snake and a pleasant surprise to say the least.

Remember, quit when you get tired. You don't make many mistakes with poisonous snakes and live to tell about it. What if I thought it was a milksnake, picked it up, and it was a coral snake? That would not be a good thing.

Cruising the roads, you can never tell what you will find next. Looking ahead, you see a snake on the road. Will it be a king or just a garter snake? That is part of the thrill of the chase.

One of the first rules of snake hunting is finding a quiet road with not much traffic. Too many cars mean too many dead snakes with frustrated and discouraged snake hunters. Nothing spoils your evening like the car in front of you running over, probably on purpose, a $50 or $100 snake.

Traffic is kind of a two-edged sword. After all, if you find dead snakes on the road, you know it is a good place and you should cruise earlier or try a side road nearby. With no cars on the road to run them over, you wouldn't know they were there to start with.

Again, a road that you catch a bunch of snakes on one night will have nothing crawling on it the next. Quite frustrating at times Just when you learn the rules, they change the rules.

In the dry hot areas, like southwest Texas, listen for the windmills. There are always snakes within a short distance of a windmill. Maybe not every time you go by, but they will be there sometime. In some places, the windmills are the only water for miles and the local snakes know where that water is. They also hang around the windmills in the daytime until it gets too hot, then they go down into a hole until dark.

Equally important is to learn what kind of snakes are in the area you are hunting. One time, at just about dusk, I saw a small snake on the road. I went to pick it up but hesitated, as something did not look right. I had just caught a couple of hognose snakes and this looked like another.

However, it was coiled up and shaking its tail. I got a light and it was a massasauga rattlesnake with the same color and shape as the hognose. It could have been rather unpleasant. Most of the snakes in southwest Texas have the same color and pattern diamondbacks, massasauga, hognose, bulls, even garters and kings, so be CAREFUL!

Lose some

On one of my early trips to Texas, I didn't know the area very well but was just driving and getting lucky by finding a few things here and there. I had quite a few snakes, lizards and other critters, but was looking for more. I was in Laredo and pulled into a gas station to fill up. The attendant came out and was filling my tank. You didn't fill your own tank in those days. I asked him if he knew of anyone that had snake or reptiles locally.

"Yes," he said, "there's someone just down the block that has all kinds of critters." With his directions, I drove on over.

The building was full of all kinds of snakes, lizards, and turtles. I really didn't need anything because I had a van full of reptiles already, but you never know what you might find. There were tanks full of collared lizards for 20 cents each, king and rat snakes for 50 cents to $1 each, and a pit with a couple hundred western diamondback rattlesnakes in it. This dealer was buying these for 40 or 50 cents a pound. You just put your bags of rattlers on the scale, marked the pounds down, and then dumped them in the pit. In this way you didn't have to handle them which was smart.

I had about thirty rattlers in the van, so I didn't need any more; but it was fun to see. I was just starting to leave when I saw a large snake in a cage off to the side. Looking closer, I saw it was a very large western indigo. I hadn't caught one yet, so I decided to buy it.

When the guy took it out of the cage, I almost couldn't believe it. It was eight feet two inches and bigger around than my arm. It was the biggest indigo I had ever seen, eastern or western. The guy charged me eight dollars, but I would have paid twice that and still been happy. I had a bunch of carrying boxes with hinged lids that I kept the poisonous snakes in. I doubled some of the rattlers up and put the indigo in and put a snap on the hasp.

The boxes were made of one quarter inch plywood and were quite strong. I'd never had a rattler get loose, but this snake was very big so I drove a nail in each corner just to be sure.

I slept that night in the back of my van after I had ridden the roads for a few hours back in the boonies. I had a folding cot and was quite comfortable. I even left the doors open since there were no mosquitoes.

I don't think it would be a good idea to do that now with all the illegals running around that area but in those days, I never had any trouble. I have been stopped by the Texas Rangers a few times and they looked in all my boxes, but they never bothered me after they found out what I was doing.

The next day I caught an indigo snake, but it wasn't near as big, only six feet. I decided to put it in the box with the other one, so I used a hammer to pull the nails from the lid, took the snap off, opened the lid, and the snake was gone.

Somehow it had pushed the plywood up just enough to slide under the edge and get out. It probably got away while I was sleeping. It's hard to believe they are that strong. I'm still sick about it and it's been 45 years, not because of the money but because of my carelessness.

I did catch an eight-footer a few years later, but it was a much lighter snake.

Blair's King Snakes in Texas

One year I was hunting out near Langtry, Texas with my good friend Bob Kromer. The best snake out there is the Blair's kingsnake and neither of us had ever caught one. We each had our own car and we thought we were really going to do great. After all, two cars could double the catch.

Someone told me to hunt the Pandale Road, north of Langtry if we wanted Blairs. It was a nice long lonely dirt road, and it went for miles.

We moteled in Langtry and everyone staying there was a snake hunter. It wasn't much of a place, but snake hunters are not fussy as long as the snakes are out. Bob and I were going to leave 15 minutes apart and ride the road all night. The guy that ran the motel, store and gas station was an old herper and was always giving advice. I started to leave but he said it was too early. I just wanted to look the area over, and besides, I couldn't sit still any longer.

I hadn't gone more than three miles when there in the road was a beautiful 32-inch Blair's. The snake was gorgeous. This was going to be easy, I remembered thinking. Well, I drove and drove and never saw another snake of any kind. I'd meet Bob now and then, but he hadn't found anything either.

Finally, after four hours, we quit and returned to the motel. We decided to try one more night as long as we were here. The next morning while it was cool, we rode around together and found a Trans-Pecos copperhead in the cattle bar right at the start of the Pandale Road.

We also got a nice Trans-Pecos rat snake and a few pretty garters. That week, at least, morning cruising was better, but we wanted some more Blairs which prefer darkness. The second night, Bob left first and caught his Blairs. It was the only snake either one of us saw that night.

We went further west the next morning but didn't catch much. We did find a DOR (dead-on-road) Blairs on the way back to Langtry. It was exactly thirteen miles from Langtry because I had checked my odometer.

The guy at the motel didn't believe us. He said he had never found one more than five miles out. Well, that goes to show you that you can't believe everyone. Just maybe, he was trying to protect his favorite hunting spot.

A couple of the other guys caught a few Blairs, but I think we were a week early. It was just a bit cool and sometimes just a few degrees make all the difference. Bob caught a pretty black-tailed rattlesnake on one of his cruises and gave it to me. He didn't have any use for poisonous snakes. I kept it for quite a while until one of my girlfriends didn't like it and I gave it away. Amazing what we will do for a woman.

Bob passed through Langtry a year or so ago and said the old herper was still there, but he had quit hunting because they were now too many permits and regulations. I have never been back, but I know there are still Blairs in that area. Just recently, I ran into a guy I met out there all those years ago and he said he still finds one now and then. Maybe someday I'll return.

Texas Flood

Driving down I-10 between Beaumont and Houston one day, Jimmy Wasserman and I came to a place that looked snakey. There were three rivers (really one with two other branches), the Trinity, the Old and the Lost.

They were in a valley about a half-mile wide just before emptying into Galveston Bay. The valley was flooded. The water was up to the tops of the fence posts, and there were lots of trees and bushes sticking out of the water as far as we could see.

There was a turnoff there, so we took it looking for a place to park. We noticed a short dead-end road that went out towards the water, so we drove a little way and parked. There were rocks piled up from the guardrail to the water. This kept the river from washing the road away.

We started walking to see if any snakes were there. There were Texas rats and speckled kings laying all around the rocks. We missed quite a few as they got down under the rocks and it got to be too much work to dig them out. We just moved on to the easier ones.

It got hot as it does in Texas and the snakes went under the rocks where it was cool and they were safe. We had a canoe with us, so we decided to paddle around the flooded trees where it was cooler. It was also better than breaking leg in the rocks. We paddled over a barbed-wire fence. This was usually a pasture. There were little clumps of oak trees and bushes scattered about and everyone seemed to have a snake in it.

There would be a speckled king in one bush and a couple of Texas rats in the next one. When the water rose, they just climbed up the first thing they came to. After a few days, the water would recede and they could get back to their business. There were lots of water snakes in the bushes too, but they usually jumped in before we could get close enough.

Paddling into a small grove of oak trees, I looked up and saw a cottonmouth lying on a limb four feet up. There were some Texas rats too, but the trees were big, and I wasn't about to climb a tree with a dangerous cottonmouth in it.

I can see where the snake stories about snakes jumping out of trees and into boats comes from. We bypassed many of the snakes in the bigger trees that were too hard to climb and sought out the easy ones. We were floating in the middle of a large open space, eating a snack, when a speckled king swam up to the canoe. Since we were the only dry spot around, I gave it a lift aboard.

I told Jimmy that this looks like a good place for alligators and he said he didn't think there were any around. However, we didn't go 100 feet when there was a dead seven ft. alligator floating by. I guess I know where alligators should be.

We hunted until a storm blew in and we returned to the car. We had a total of 20 Texas rats, 15 speckled kings, a bunch of cottonmouths, and water snakes. It was a great day!

We went back there a few days later and caught quite a few more. Then we went to southwestern Texas to dry out for a few days. We should have stayed in the east because when we returned to the river, the water was almost gone. Now, we only caught snakes in the rocks.

When they are crawling, catch them, they will probably not be there tomorrow. We did get an extra treat on this last visit when the water was low. Along the edge of the river, we noticed little rings of water around almost of the trees. Within these rings were dozens of mud bugs, crayfish or crawdads or whatever you call them. Apparently, they dig the rings to hold the water longer. We had a large cooler in the canoe with us, so we just carried it next to a tree and cupping our hands we scooped up hundreds of them and filled the cooler in a few minutes.

Back at my grandmother's house, we cooked up the tasty little lobsters and ate our fill. These Texas crayfish were much bigger than the Connecticut ones, and they pinched harder too.

Rattlesnake

I was hunting with my old buddy Jerry Walls up near the Okeetee Plantation off Tillman Road. It was the first time I had hunted in South Carolina. I parked the car and we decided to split up to cover more ground. The area was posted, so I just walked along the highway up one side and back down the other to the car. I managed to catch one small red rat snake. When I got back to the car, Jerry was not there yet.

As I waited, two guys in a truck pulled up to check on me. They said the area was posted. I said I knew, and I was just looking along the road. They said that was okay. We talked snakes a few minutes and just as they were leaving, Jerry, who was just down the road a little way (maybe just inside the posted area), started to shout. I am kind of deaf and he hadn't seen the guys yet. "Frank! Rattlesnake! Rattlesnake!"

He hadn't taken a hook with him and he needed a hand. Now the guys knew where he was, but they said to go ahead and help him since it sounded like he needed help. By the way, if you stop at the Okeetee headquarters, they will give you permission to snake hunt there. They were nice guys.

White Lie

I was always honest with my wife except for one time when I had to tell her a white lie. On one of our annual trips to the Carolinas, I had a problem. As soon as we crossed into South Carolina from Georgia (Georgia is closed to non-venomous snake hunting), I had some good places to look. There were pieces of tin around a few billboards where I had been catching snakes for almost 40 years.

At the first piece of tin, there was a nice big copperhead under it. This was a good start. The piece of tin was 20-feet-long and 2 feet wide. The snake was hot and kept going back and forth making it hard to catch. There were also briars in the way. I finally got it on a snake hook and into a bag.

It was pretty annoyed by now. I knotted the bag and started back to the car. The vines and briars were thick, and I had to force my way through. The bag snagged on the briars and I received a scratched kneecap or so I thought. I got to the car, put the snake in a box, and drove up to the next piece of tin.

At this piece, there was nothing. About then, my knee started to throb. I figured I had a thorn sticking in it. I rolled up my pants leg and saw my knee was puffed up and oozing a little blood, all in less than ten minutes.

Well, that was no thorn. The copperhead must have scratched me with a fang when I got tangled in the briars. Now I wasn't about to mess up my snake hunting vacation over a little scratch from a copperhead, so I didn't tell my wife. She wouldn't have been too happy. She's now my ex-wife. She still doesn't know about my knee until she reads this. Anyway, I told her I banged it on a log. It swelled a little, got black and blue, but it didn't hurt, although I limped for a few days. I managed to get through the trip okay. We caught a lot of snakes and had a good time. In a week, I was as good as new.

Hardeeville Reds

On one of my early trips to Hardeeville, South Carolina, I was with Jerry Walls. He had been there before, and his knowledge of the area would save time. We arrived there late in the evening having driven in from Fort Lauderdale. We did find a few snakes on the trip, but I was still excited about hunting the South Carolina low country.

We checked into a dinky motel the one Jerry normally stayed in. They were tired of loose snakes from careless snake hunters. Since it was still light, Jerry thought we should take a walk. Hardeeville wasn't very big then and we just went a few blocks from the motel when Jerry recognized a snakey place. It was right across from a gas station. There were houses and buildings all around it. It didn't look very good to me.

I could see a chimney sticking up in the bushes and Jerry said there were some tin sheets near it. He added, however, that he hadn't caught anything there in a few years. As we stepped off the road, we saw a round sign six feet in diameter lying partially in the water. We figured we should move it to dry ground because we thought no self-respecting snake would reside under a wet piece of tin. I picked it up and there were two nice corn snakes under it. So much for what I know.

We continued toward the chimney to see if the other tin was still there. It was. We caught six more beautiful reds under the tin. The tin had not been flipped for at least two years and was pinned to the ground by honeysuckle. For years afterward, we went back to this place but never caught another snake there. For that particular evening, the conditions had been just right.

Feisty Copperhead

I just recently took a short trip to North and South Carolina to visit with some friends and to snake hunt a little. Well, we went out a few times and caught a few corns, kings and copperheads.

Unfortunately, there was a heat wave going on, and it was too hot under the tin for the snakes to stay there very late in the morning. We had to wait until later in the day when it cooled down.

Nevertheless, we had a nice visit and a good time. I decided to head back to Florida. In southern South Carolina, I have a few special pieces of tin signs that I have been catching snakes under for 40 years. Some of them are almost rusted away, but some of this tm is still going strong.

I checked the place where Jerry Walls and I caught four corn snakes the first time I hunted up there, but there was nothing left. Another place gone. I went down the road and parked by some other tin sign where the copperhead bit me five years before and there was another copperhead there.

I have probably caught 20 copperheads there over the years. I hung a bag open over a bush and picked the snake up with my tongs, but the tongs jammed, and the snake slipped out. I tried again and it slipped out again. I backed up a little because the snake was thrashing around in the leaves, all upset. I was keeping my eye on the snake as I worked on the tongs. The snake started crawling towards me. I backed up a little more and the snake kept coming.

I have heard hundreds of stories about snakes chasing people but never believed many of them. I decided to see just what the snake would do. I thought I might be between the snake and its hole, so I moved a few steps to my right and the snake came after me again. I moved to the left and the snake came that way. It was out to get me.

It is a good thing they are not fast. I stepped back over a six-inch high log, the snake crawled up on it and struck at me. I was out of reach and it struck at me several more times.

"Enough of this," I thought. I had the tongs working again. I picked the snake up, dropped it in the bag, tied it shut, and went back to the car. I had survived my first snake attack. That snake chased me over 25 feet. There seems to be a family of really mean snakes right in that area and I will be more careful next time I go there. Bill Tudor was bitten by a canebrake rattler not far from there and he died from that bite.

Claxton Rattlesnake Roundup

My friend Dan Wells from Tennessee and I were on the way to snake hunt in the Carolinas when we decided to check out the rattlesnake roundup in Claxton, Georgia. It was one of the big events in the area. Claxton is famous for the roundup and fruitcakes.

The roundup was held in a large warehouse with all the usual contests - largest snake, most snakes caught, milking, bagging and, of course, a rattlesnake roundup queen. For sale were deep-fried rattlesnake meat and snakeskin products - belts, wallets, and buckles. There were over 400 rattlers in a big pit, and it was rather impressive. I didn't see a non-poisonous snake there. We didn't stay very long because we wanted to get hunting. However, we did meet a guy named John who said he would take us out and find us some rattlers. It turned out he had won most of the prizes the last several years. He was busy at the roundup and we said we would stop on our way back from the Carolinas.

We didn't do well in the Carolinas as things were changing for the worse. There were too many hunters and restrictions. Returning to Georgia, we looked up John and, as promised, he showed us around. It's not hard to get a snake hunter to go snake hunting.

We drove to some open woods and started walking. John has a different way of hunting. He catches most of his snakes in the winter. Since it doesn't get that cold in Georgia, John digs them out of gopher tortoise holes where the rattlers den up during cold spells.

Most of the other hunters here used a length of garden hose that they pushed down into the hole and then pour a little gasoline into the hose. The fumes would make the snakes come out where they were easily caught. This method burned the snakes' lungs and they would die in a month or so.

Today gassing is illegal almost everywhere, and it should be. I never did it. It also killed the tortoises. John dug his snakes out and stockpiled them for months before the roundup. John did carry a piece of hose, but he used it as a stethoscope. He covered the end of the hose to be inserted into the hole with screening to keep out the dirt. He then pushed the hose down the hole and listened. If a tortoise was in the hole, you could hear it thumping around; but if a snake was there, you would hear a swishing sound. This sure saved a lot of needless digging since some of these holes went down 20 feet. John said he has caught many as six rattlers in one hole.

We only got one rattler that day since the place was pretty well hunted out. He also probably didn't want to show us any of his best spots. He did have a lot of holes dug around there. This was hard work but more humane than gassing. He had half a freezer full of dead rattlers that had been road killed and a few that had died in captivity. I bought their skins for my snakeskin projects. It had been fun to see how someone else hunted rattlesnakes. It sure involved more digging than I cared to do. John could have been a gravedigger judging by some of his excavations. I prefer catching my rattlers sitting near a hole.

Bill Tudor

I was walking along a canal one day up near Fort Piece, Florida, over 100 miles from where I was living when I saw a guy coming from the opposite direction. When he got closer, I saw It was Bill Tudor.

Bill and I seem to be in the same place at the same time quite often. We never really went hunting together but we have ended up in the same vicinity several times, mostly in the Carolinas. I remember one time sitting in a restaurant in South Carolina on a cold morning. We were waiting for it to get warm enough to start hunting. Bill would go outside, put his hand on the sidewalk, come in and say, "It's still too cool."

We would wait another half hour and he would do it again. Finally, he said, "It's warm enough" and we would all take off in a mad dash to see who would catch the first snake. It was never me.

A few years later, I was driving down a lonely road out in West Texas. I had not seen a car in an hour, which is how I liked it. There on the horizon came a car going slowly like me. I saw it stop, a guy got out, and picked up a snake off the road, so I knew what he was doing.

We finally pulled up opposite each other and stopped. He asked about having much luck. I said, "A few, how about you?"

He said, "I got a few too."

I said, "Bill?"

He said, "Frank?"

It is a small world and we were hundreds of miles from home.

A few weeks later, I checked into a small hotel, a couple hundred miles from where Bill and I had accidentally met and there he was again. He was recovering from a bite he had gotten two days before from a Trans-Pecos copperhead. He did not look very good. He had big blood blisters all over his arms and chest.

That species of copperhead has a large amount of neurotoxin as well as hemotoxin venom, but he never went to a doctor. He didn't trust them. Two days later, he was out riding the roads and catching snakes again. Nine months later, he was hunting in South Carolina, was bitten by a canebrake rattlesnake, and died in less than an hour. They got him to an ambulance, but he never made it to the hospital.

I just recently heard that they have found some canebreaks that have large amounts of the neurotoxin venom, same as the Trans-Pecos. You do not survive many bites of that kind. Bill was probably still weak from the first bite or just becoming more sensitive with each bite.

Do not take any more chances than you have to. I used to pin everything, now I almost never touch the snakes. I use my tongs to lift them with my hook and drop them in a bag. Life is too short, and the bites HURT!

A bunch of us snake hunters were staying in the same motel in South Carolina one spring and sometimes we all used to go out together to really cover an area. Bill had a thing he used to do. He would find a rattler, copperhead, or cottonmouth on a cool day when the snakes weren't warmed up, and slide his hand slowly under the snake from the back, lift it up, and then drop it in a bag.

"It will not bite. It is tame," he would always say. I have seen him do this a dozen times, but a Southern copperhead finally got him one day.

I tried it once and it worked, but it was the last time. It was too hard on my nerves.

It's Great To Be Young

A former girlfriend, Pauline Gammon, and I used to go road cruising for snakes in Florida. Pauline wasn't into snakes too much, but I was gradually breaking her into this activity. One day, she suggested we go north to South Carolina for the weekend and go snake hunting in the area where I used to spring hunt. I agreed largely because I'm easy to get along with and I like to hunt snakes.

Well, I worked all day Friday at the orange grove until 5 pm. I packed a few things and had supper. Then I drove 15 miles to the bowling alley where Pauline and I were in a league that started at 7 p.m.

We bowled three games and finished at 9 p.m. and left for South Carolina. I drove all night, it was exactly 500 miles, while my co-pilot slept. We got there a little after 9 a.m., had some breakfast, and got a motel room. Pauline said she wanted to sleep, but I could go hunting if I wanted.

Well, I went up the road a little way to a spot I used to hunt years ago. It had just been burned over and it looked good. It was good, I found a couple of kings and corn snakes by stump holes. It was approaching lunchtime and since I work up an appetite in a hurry, I headed back toward the car. Walking along, I noticed a small patch of red in a hole in the ground. It turned out to be a red rat snake.

The hole was so small that I couldn't get my hand into it. I poked the snake, but it wouldn't move. I then cut some roots with my pocketknife so I could get to the snake. I finally worked it out of the hole, and it was the biggest red I had ever seen - six feet to the inch. I was admiring my catch when I looked back at the hole, and there was another red the same size. Bagging them both, I headed back to the motel. It was a super morning.

Pauline was also ready for lunch. She picked a restaurant, and there was Bill Tudor again. Also, with him was another old buddy, Larry Robertson. After lunch, Larry saw the big reds and just had to have them. He owned a pet shop in Miami. Those two snakes paid for the whole trip and then some.

After lunch, Pauline wanted to go hunting so I drove out to the country when I came to a place where I had remembered Jerry Walls catching three rattlers a few years ago. I stopped. There was nothing there but an old house trailer across the road where someone had removed the frame and sides. Now just the roof remained, a nice big tin roof. We went over and I told Pauline I'd pick it up and she should catch what's under it. I picked up one end, just barely, and there were three nice king snakes there.

"Grab them!" I said.

She just stood there.

"They might bite me," she said.

No wonder I didn't marry her. I couldn't lift and grab at the same time, so I let it down. The roof was out in the open. If there wasn't a hole under it, the kings couldn't get away. I found a strong stick and went back to try again. I lifted and Pauline propped the roof up with the stick. I crawled under and started grabbing. She at least held the bag open. We propped up the other end and got two more kings for a total of five.

We rode around a while and caught a few more snakes. Returning to the motel, I slept till supper. The night was cool, too cool for road hunting. In the morning, we set our compass south checking a few of my special places and finding a few more reds and kings. I dropped Pauline off after the 500-mile trip back and went home to bed.

I had to work the next day. The next weekend, I made the same trip again with a male friend. Unfortunately, the weather had changed, and it was too hot. We only caught one red rat, but I did get more sleep.

Hay, Piles, and Burns

One year, I was in Hardeeville, South Carolina for the spring snake hunt. There was a bunch of us all staying at the same motel. At that time, we mostly hunted the burned-over woodlands. There wasn't much tin for us to look under or we didn't know where any of it was located. It was a cool rainy day and we knew there would be no snakes crawling.

I finally got bored of just hanging around, decided to take a drive, and look the country over. Just maybe, I might find a place worth hunting when the weather improved. A few miles outside of town, the rain let up. In spite of the cold, I decided to walk and stretch my legs a little. A highway crew had mowed the side of the road a month before when the grass must have been quite high. There were now piles of grass looking like mowed hay scattered on both sides of the road. Some piles were quite large. As I walked with my snake hook, I started digging idly through the piles.

The first pile had a mouse nest in it. That's always a good sign. The second pile had a nest with mice in it, an even better sign. The third pile had a nice fat king snake under it.

Amazingly, it was dry under the hay. I had just finished reading Kauffeld's book "Snakes and Snake Hunting" that talked about finding snakes under piles of grass along Paynes

Prairie in Florida. That reading may be what prompted me to examine these piles. I caught a few more kings and a beautiful red rat snake before it started to rain again. Those were the only snakes caught that day by anyone.

The next day was sunny and warm and we went back to hunting the burns which were usually more productive.

When conditions were right you could walk up to a good stump hole, and there would be two or three kings, reds, copperheads or even rattlesnakes lying around soaking up the sun. You never knew what to expect, but you could usually catch everything.

They don't burn as much as they used to, but they should. Fires keep naturally caused fires from becoming uncontrollable. I never remember seeing any dead snakes after a fire. Some box turtles suffered and many of the turtles had scars on their shells from the fires burning over them quickly.

I have found a few dead yellow rat snakes in Florida when a fire completely engulfed trees the snakes were in. Snakes that go down a hole survive. I have even seen snakes lying just a few feet from a smoking stump. Green grass quickly sprouts in these burns and it is easier to walk when the excess brush has been eliminated. By burning every year, the fires never get very hot and the big trees don't really suffer at all.

You Can't Catch Them All

I took a job one summer near Copake, New York taking care of a small estate. There, I caught both spotted and black hognose snakes, garters and milksnakes.

I met one of the local guys who told me where a rattlesnake den was, and I set out to find it. I figured it would be another wild snake chase. I drove around and around and finally found a place that matched the guy's description. On the other side of the dirt road on which I had parked was a barbed-wire fence with six timber rattlesnakes hanging on it, dead. That sight kind of spoiled my whole day.

Much of the time, I'm a day late and a dollar short as the saying goes. I walked around for a couple of hours but saw nothing. I returned a few times, but it was late in the summer. If there were any rattlers left, they had all dispersed. I left for Florida before they had gone back to the den for the winter, so I never did know if there were any more there. Maybe, I'll go look one of these days.

Just before leaving for Florida, I happened to go down to a little pond on this estate and it was full of spotted newts. Using a minnow net, I caught over 300 in just a few minutes. I've never seen them so thick before or since. I dropped them off at

Gordon Johnston's in New Jersey since he said he could use them.

On the same trip back, I stopped right at the Virginia/North Carolina border at a snakey looking place. While walking the road's shoulder, two cottonmouths took off and went into a drainage pipe under the road. Nothing I could do would make them come out. I could almost maneuver them to the other side of the culvert, but when I ran over, they would return to the middle. They weren't worth much in those days anyway. That is as far north as cottonmouths range, but these two were fat and sassy.

While out in West Texas one time, I noticed a train track parallel to the highway I was driving. As I drove along, I glanced at the trestles. Bridges are always good for snakes and so are trestles if they are built right. At one trestle, I saw something hanging down. I decided to check it out. The thing hanging down was exactly what I thought it was, a snake's shedded skin. There must have been a dozen sheds. I poked and peered into cracks and crevices, before I finally found one small Emory's rat snake. I now knew the species of snake from which the sheds had come. Every trestle had lots of sheds but no live snakes.

I guessed they were way back in the rocks. I should have gone back after dark, but I moved on and got to finding something else. I'm sure if the trestles are still there, the snakes are too. You just have to be there at the right time.

Frank Over the Years

Starting with Frank's parents, Frank and Ellen Weed were often used as models on various sporting, hunting, and fishing magazine covers

Frank doing an educational presentation on big cats

Diana Maas with Buzzy

Frank and friends catching a wild gator

Frank with some big cats

Frank with some big cats

Frank with some big cats

Frank with some big cats

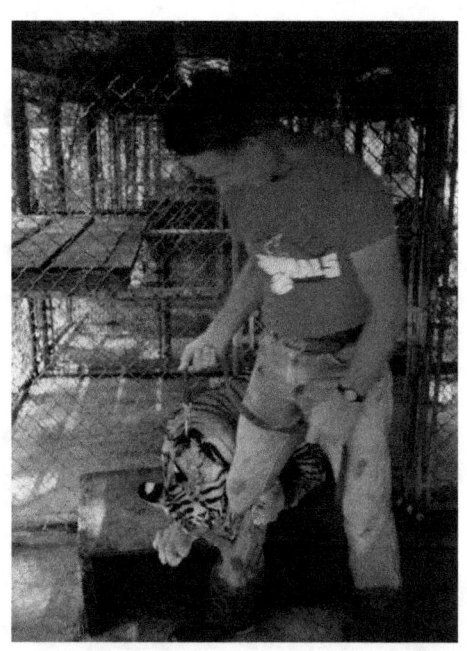

Frank still has the knack on catching fish

Still catching a fish by hand

Frank with an 8-foot road kill indigo snake

Pinned Down by a Sign

I was snake hunting up in the Carolinas with my buddy Jerry Walls and we were walking along the highway catching a few snakes when I saw a metal sign lying in the bushes. It did not look too heavy, but I had all I could do to lift it up. Jerry wasn't nearby and when I looked under the sign, there were several king snakes resting. Kings were a good catch, so I grabbed a couple with one hand while I held the sign up with the other. I got a little greedy and tried to grab another nice one, but I reached too far. The sign fell on top of me. There I was with just my head sticking out, not hurt but I could not get out from under the sign without letting go of the snakes which I was not going to do.

Jerry finally showed up and when he stopped laughing, he picked the sign off of me. We caught a few more snakes under the same sign and continued our hunting. We still have a good laugh about this whenever I see him.

Strange Bedfellows

Skeet Johns and I took a fast trip to North Carolina to pick up some white-tailed deer fawns from a game farm. My father needed eight of them. We crated them in the back of our pickup truck and headed back down to Florida.

Skeet had not driven yet and around Darlington, South Carolina, I got tired. I always liked to camp out on trips although it's not as safe anymore. Anyway, I found a nice quiet spot behind some trees and parked.

We fed the fawns some milk from a bottle. Feeding them from a bottle gets them tame quickly. Chores done, we got ready to sleep. There was a nice big tangle of honeysuckle vines right by the truck. The vines were two or three feet thick and thick enough to support us.

"This looks like a good place to sleep," I said. Skeet agreed. We spread our sleeping bags on top of the vines and climbed in. It was like lying on a spring mattress, very comfortable and I slept like a log. It smelled good too.

At dawn, we got up, fed the fawns again, and got ready to leave. As I went to get my sleeping bag, I heard a piece of tin crackle under my foot. There had been a house or barn there at one time, but there was nothing left but the tin roof. I just had to look under it. When I moved the vines off the tin, there were two big copperheads under it. We had been sleeping right on top of them all night. It was probably a good thing we had such a comfortable place to sleep since we did not toss and turn during the night.

Anyway, my luck was still working.

Three Kings

On our way back to Florida after a successful snake hunting trip to South Carolina, Jerry Walls and I were looking for more snakes and critters. I like to play hunches and I have a feel about places. More often than not, I am right.

As we were going through Georgia, we came upon a sign along the road that said "King Swamp". Well, we were looking for king snakes, so I said, "Let's try it!"

I pulled off the road at a wide spot and parked. Jerry opened the door and stepped out right on a king snake. How's that for service?

I got out and walked around the car to look at it and there was another king. As we were standing there admiring the snakes, Jerry said, "There's another one!" He caught that one, too.

Three kings in less than a minute. Do you know we hunted around there for half an hour and never saw another snake? I stopped there off and on for several years and never caught another snake. I guess I used up all my luck on the first bunch.

A Smart Bird

When I lived near Ft. Lauderdale in Davie, it was pretty much country. We thought we lived in the sticks, but now the sticks are much farther out and, for the most part, really don't exist anymore. We had to be in the country because our yard was full of bears, mountain lions, leopards, deer, and all kinds of other critters. My parents were in the animal business. We finally had to move way out to Immokalee, Florida to get away from progress.

In our new place, I noticed a mocking bird building a nest in one of our orange trees. A couple of weeks later, as I was walking through the yard, a mocking bird flew over to me, fluttered in front of my face, and flew over to the orange tree. Then she did the same thing again. I finally figured out that she wanted me to follow her, so I went over to the tree. Just then, I remembered the previously built nest. When I got there, a big five-foot yellow rat snake was eating one of her babies. I caught the snake which seemed to be a relief to the bird. Her actions saved most of her babies.

How did that bird know that I caught snakes? How did she know that I would not eat her babies? Who knows? Kind of makes you wonder. Animals and birds are a lot smarter than people give them credit for.

Croc Catching

When Bill Haast sold his serpentarium in Miami, he sold off many reptiles he didn't need for his new place in Punta Gorda.

Bruce Swedick from Maryland bought Cookie, the 13-foot, 800 pound crocodile. He wanted my father, me and six other guys to help him remove it from the pit. I went into the pit and got a rope around Cookie and eight guys pulled and I pushed. Finally, we got the impressive beastie out of the pit.

There were some people waiting to get into the crocodile less pit as there were thousands of coins that people had thrown in for 20 plus years. Someone had bid for the rights to the coins and he got over a bathtub full.

A while later, Bruce bought a croc from Gatorama located near Clewiston, Florida. At Gatorama, a small lake had been dug and divided equally with crocs on one side and gators on the other. The croc that Bruce had purchased had escaped into the gators' side and Bruce couldn't catch it. Bruce called me for help and I always enjoyed a challenge. I brought my heavy rod and treble hooks and two friends.

There was a covered walkway over the lake and you could gaze at the gators and crocs on both sides. There were over 100 big alligators on one side. It wasn't anyplace to paddle a canoe as someone had suggested. I may be crazy but I'm not stupid.

I walked around the gators side to see if I could find the croc. While I was in the wooded backside of the lake, a seven-foot gator charged me from the lake. As I back stepped quickly, I almost tripped over the gator's nest, a big pile of leaves and grass. Once I was past the nest, the gator's charge and threat stopped. She was only defending her nest. I still had not seen the croc, so I went back to the walkway to visually search with the others.

From the gift shop, I borrowed binoculars. Gator heads filled the lenses. I scanned back and forth and thought I saw the croc, but it went under. I kept focused on the same spot and, in a few minutes, it came up. It was the croc and down it went again. The croc seemed to know I was looking at it. The gators did not react to my staring but as soon as I made eye contact with the croc it submerged. The good thing was it kept surfacing in the same spot. Note: gators don't do this.

Since I knew the croc's location, I decided to try to hook it. This would be tricky since gators were everywhere. My first 75-yard cast hooked a turtle. I made another cast and thought I had snagged a root, but the root started moving. The croc almost pulled me in as the drag was too tight. I eased the drag and held on. When the big pointed-snout popped up, everyone came running.

Not liking crocs, my friend Diana Maas helped by taking pictures. That was all she was willing to do. Mark Ray and Bruce managed to rope the croc and we dragged it onto the bank. I removed my shirt and covered the croc's eyes. If they can't see, crocs will quit resisting. We got it all tied up and loaded it in Bruce's van.

Bruce went north to Maryland since he had a show to do. This had been his last chance to get this croc, and he was grateful. I'm always glad to help. Plus, I like the fun and excitement. Besides, on the way home, I caught a five-foot diamondback rattler crossing the highway. That made it a nice profitable day.

In The Movies

I used to hunt along an abandoned railroad bed along Route 29 below Immokalee. There used to be many diamondback rattlesnakes, big Brooks kings, pigmy rattlesnakes, cottonmouths, red and yellow rat snakes, a really great place to hunt.

I went hunting out there one day with a friend and we caught eight nice diamondbacks. I went out with Dad a couple days later and we got 13 rattlers. The very next day, we caught 10 more. This was the area where we went deer hunting with our dogs and we were trying to give our dogs a better chance of surviving the hunting season by removing the diamondbacks.

I took them all down to Miami to sell, but the dealer was overstocked and said he couldn't use any. I returned home and had to figure out what to do with 31 big rattlesnakes. Almost at the very moment I walked into the house, the phone rang. A guy said he was making a movie and needed a bunch of rattlesnakes. Someone had given him my name and said that I might be able to help him. I was elated.

"Stanley" was the name of the movie, and it did very well. I had started a regular job about that time, so I wasn't able to work on the movie much.

My mother and father became the snake handlers on the set. The story was loosely based on my lifestyle and I had worked with this writer before. The lead actor, Chris Robertson, carried a rattlesnake named Stanley around his neck throughout the movie. I, of course, wasn't that crazy

In the movie, the lead character used to give and sell snakes to people. When some of these people killed the snakes, Chris threw rattlesnakes on them. These people died, as did Chris in the movie. Mom and Dad had bit parts. The movie grossed SIX million dollars the first month and making the producers happy.

We also worked the gators and snakes in a low-budget film "Death Curse of Tartu". I think they spent only $16,000 on the whole film. They used local actors and shot it in four weekends.

In that film, Dad was "killed" by a 17-foot anaconda. We did some stunt work in "Frogs" with Ray Milland. They had a few scenes that didn't come out right, because the actors were afraid of our critters. My father replaced one of the actors by wearing a bald wig. He waded into a little pond where he was "killed" by a gator. There was much thrashing and splashing.

Dad put one arm over the gator's jaws and one under which made it look like his arm was in the gator's mouth. It looked realistic and they got the scene done with one take. My mother doubled for one of the actresses by wearing a wig and a dress. She had to fall into a pond and come out covered with leeches, pieces of rubber snakes were used. Then she was bitten by a rattlesnake. They needed two takes because the first time Mom fell in, her dress floated up and she pushed it down.

Making movies was fun, if you could get beyond the slow-moving parts.

Rattlers with Personalities

Hunting the old railroad bed near our house, I checked a piece of tin I had placed there a few years before. Lifting it, I found two large diamondbacks and 20 baby rattlers. I caught the two big ones and about half of the babies. They had scattered in every direction and, since they had very little value, I didn't try hard to find them. I thought I'd try to raise a couple of the babies and see if I could tame one.

Eastern diamondbacks are high-strung and don't do well in captivity. Your best chance to keep and tame one is by starting with a newborn. They don't know anything yet. I gave them some time to adjust to a big aquarium. When I thought these babies had calmed down, I put some mice in with them and watched. Most of them ate the mice, but later a few of the babies regurgitated them. The ones that didn't eat the mice or couldn't keep them down, I released. I ended up with four babies that ate and didn't mind being handled.

A doctor friend of mine wanted a few baby rattlers to raise, so I gave him two. He had them for a while and then decided to remove their venom glands to be a little safer. A few weeks after the operation, he put a mouse in the cage. The snake struck and the mouse died. The doctor knew the procedure wasn't a success, and he didn't freehand feed either of the babies anymore.

I decided to keep one baby which I named Buzzy. Buzzy did really well for almost three years. I could freehand it carefully and it never tried to strike. However, it readily killed mice and later rats as it got bigger. Typically, Buzzy would bite the mouse and then wait in the corner a few minutes until the poison worked. Then it would crawl over and touch the mouse. If it moved, Buzzy would wait a few more minutes. When the mouse was dead for sure, Buzzy would eat it. Buzzy was crazy about cotton rats. He would even eat road-killed ones. If I caught a cotton rat, I usually killed it. They are slightly immune to the venom and would sit around the cage half dead for too long. White rats always died in a minute or two.

The next summer, I caught another baby rattler and it and Buzzy became good cage mates. A year later, I caught another baby, but this one must have had a disease. Within two weeks, all three of my young rattlers were dead. At that time, Buzzy was almost four feet long. I missed his neat personality and his never biting me.

I had another neat rattlesnake that I caught in Texas. It was a beautiful, pink-banded rock rattlesnake. I kept this snake in a cage next to my TV. One day while watching TV, I noticed the snake suddenly started dashing around and tapping on the glass. I couldn't imagine what its trouble was until I realized a white mouse was behind my chair. The snake could see it perfectly well, but I couldn't. I rewarded the snake's attentiveness by giving it the mouse. The snake was content for the rest of the day.

Bruce Bednar

Bruce Bednar, he helped catch the 23-foot python that was under a house in Fort Lauderdale and was featured on "Rescue 911," a fellow snake hunter and I often hunt the same area. There are miles and miles of unoccupied roads crisscrossing a failed housing development where we ride around and around and back and forth.

Bruce rides a motorcycle most of the time and covers about twice as much ground as I do. I drive sometimes 20 or 30 miles in an evening. Some nights we will not catch anything, but not very often. Other nights, he will catch three corn snakes and I will catch one. The next night, it will be reversed. It is just the luck of the draw or something like being in the right place at the right time.

I would see him up ahead of me, and before I could turn in a different direction, I would find a corn snake right where he had just gone by only a minute before. He too, has caught them right behind me.

It almost seemed like the snakes lay on the side of the road until a car passes, then they head across. However, there is almost no traffic in this area. Most nights I never see another vehicle except for Bruce.

Morris

My stories are mostly about snakes and alligators, but I thought I would relate a few other tales about what I used to do when I wasn't catching snakes.

Dad used to have many people come out and take pictures of his cougars, leopards, bobcats even lions and tigers. He was the cats Cat Man. I was the Snake Man. I worked and lived with the cats and we always had a trailer full of young cougars or tigers or something, but I always had my snake room.

Morris was one of the cougar kittens born at our ranch and raised on a bottle. He was very tame and even used to sleep with me at times. One day after he grew up, he decided he did not like me anymore. I could never handle him after that and at almost 200 pounds, I did not want to try. Dad had to lead him on a rope out to the filming area for the photo shoots.

One day, we were filming at the far end of our property and we took Morris in a cage in the back of our van since it was a long walk. Morris would only work/pose for about half an hour before he got tired. We were taking him back to get another model.

Dad opened the sliding door of the cage, Morris jumped in and then he jumped out, right over Dad and headed into the thick woods. I took off after him. I found him in a bunch of bushes but all I had on me was a short leash about ten feet long. Morris had never been loose before and was a little disturbed. Snarling, he came towards me. I backed around a little tree and made a loop in the short rope and tossed it around his head. He came around the tree and I got on the other side and he could not quite reach me. If the rope had been a foot shorter, I might have been bitten.

All this time, I was yelling for Dad who finally came and led Morris back to the van. He did nip me on my leg a year later, but you can hardly see the scars now. Morris was one of the most photographed cougars in the country. He was on a poster, postcards and even on the cover of a book put out by the National Geographic Magazine. Morris lived to the ripe old age of twenty-two.

Lobo

As I said, my parents were animal people. My mother liked any kind of animal, but my father liked cats, big cats and cougars in particular. We had up to 35 cougars at one time along with a few lions, tigers, and leopards. I put up with them all but I still preferred snakes.

I had a timber wolf named Lobo that I was fond of. I used my mom Ellen with Lobo when he tried to eat me one time. I had her take him around in the car with me until he decided he was the alfa wolf. He started giving me a hard time, so I did not handle him much.

One day, I was at the compound doing something and my mother started to take Lobo for a walk. He loved women, and Mom did not know I was out and about. Lobo saw me and came after me. You would be surprised at how fast a 150-pound wolf can drag a 120-pound woman and you would also be surprised how fast I could run with a 150-pound wolf chasing me. I had to jump up on a six-foot tall cage to get away.

Mother finally got him calmed down and put him away. I never could handle him after that!

Wildlife Officer

My old friend Charlie Fitch from Mamaroneck, New York and I were out hunting along the Tamiami Trail one evening. We were only a few miles southeast of Naples, Florida. The canal paralleling the Trail was about 40 feet wide and eight feet deep and the hydrilla weed filled the canal solid right up to the top. It was also full of water snakes, mostly banded. There were hundreds of them. We walked along the bank and caught quite a few, but then we could not reach any more when it became too deep to wade.

I finally got a bright idea. We had been fishing earlier at the Naples Pier and had our rods in the car. I caught a frog and tied the line around its middle, no hook, and cast out into the canal. While dragging the frog along the grass, it would bump into a snake and the snake would grab the frog. If l reeled it in quickly, the snake couldn't let go of the frog and I'd swing the snake in and grab it. The snake would let the frog go and I'd bag the snakes. They were mostly two to three feet long. It worked great. We caught almost every snake that grabbed the frog. The snakes own curved-backward teeth held it on.

We finally got tired and figured we had enough and were getting ready to return to the motel. It was probably one o'clock in the morning, when a Wildlife Officer pulled up and asked to see our fishing licenses. I said we were not fishing we were catching snakes. There I was standing there with a fishing rod in my hand.

He said "Oh?"

I told him to watch. I made a cast in the dark. I had already taken my headlight off. I reeled a little, felt a bite, reeled in fast, swung the snake up, grabbed it, and put it in a bag.

I wish I could have a picture of the expression on his face. He just turned around, got back in his truck and drove away! Yes, we actually did have fishing licenses.

Snakeskin Stuff

Some of the snakes I used in my shows at schools and fairs would die and I would skin and salt them. I sent some to be tanned and they came back quite nice. I used them for decorations at the shows.

A friend made a hand-tooled wallet that I liked, so I tried to make one. It came out fine except for the carved design. I decided to glue a piece of the snakeskin over where the carving was, lace it up, and I had a beautiful wallet.

I had all these pretty tanned skins, so I started making a few more wallets and belt buckles to give as Christmas presents. Some of the people who received these presents wanted some for their friends. After a while, I had a small business going. It was something to do in my spare time. After all, you can't snake hunt all the time.

I picked up road-killed snakes and some of the reptile dealers in Miami saved some of their dead stuff for me. I used to get all kinds of exotic stuff boas, pythons, cobras, etc. I started tanning the skins myself with Tannit Hide Tanning Solution to save money. It works great and is easy to use.

Salt, alum, and glycerin will work but not nearly as good. Just about anything you can make out of leather, you can cover with snakeskin and have an instant design. I was making snakeskin covered belts, buckles, hatbands, earrings, wallets, key cases, and knife cases. I even covered a few hats, purses, and boots with snakeskins.

My wife, Sandy wrote three articles that were published in Leather Crafters Journal about how I made things covered with snakeskin. She even photographed the pictures used in the articles. They looked very good and we received positive responses to them. I do not make much stuff anymore. I am getting a little arthritis and that takes all the fun out of it.

Wiggly

I took a bunch of snakes down to Miami to sell one day. A dealer there was paying more than anyone else. The prices were good, but the guy was a little short on cash and wanted to know if I would take a baby python as part payment.

Pythons were just becoming popular, and I was thinking about getting one anyway. I picked out a pretty one and received the rest in cash. This Burmese python was about 16 inches long, nice and chubby. He used to curl up in my hand when I watched television and would never move. However, if someone else held him, he would wiggle around and never stay still, hence the name Wiggly.

He was always calm with me and he never bit anyone the 15 years I had him. I used him in dozens of shows and hundreds of people held him. I took him to schools and when he got to be around 15 feet long and 100 pounds, it would take ten kids to hold him for a picture.

I started feeding him mice and baby chicks then moved up to rats and rabbits as he got bigger. As he grew bigger, he would even eat fresh road kills, rabbits, squirrels, and various birds. This saved on the feeding bill. White rabbits were five or six dollars apiece and he would eat one or two a week. On this diet, he got to be pretty hefty.

People gave me a few more Burmese pythons and I kept them for a couple of years until they started eating me out of house and home. Then I sold them and just kept Wiggly.

One cold spell, yes it does get cold in Florida, Wiggly did not get on his heating unit and caught a cold and died. This happened before I knew he was even sick. He was 17 feet and well over 100 pounds. I still miss him, he did not have a mean bone in his body.

Mom

Some of the snakes I catch lay eggs in their cages before I sell them. I usually hatch and release these to keep the supply up. They also have a better chance of hatching in captivity than in the wild, what with all the beasties out there that like to eat eggs — raccoons, opossums, skunks, armadillos, and lately fire ants. It is a wonder any of them hatch. I still hatch and release 50 to 100 every year.

One time I had about a dozen king snake eggs laid in a cage. I placed them on damp newspaper and put them in a one-pound coffee can with a few small holes in it. I put it in a cupboard over the stove where it would get a little heat. Periodically, I sprinkled a little water on them when they started to dry out.

One morning while I was eating breakfast, my mother Ellen let out a yell. She had gone to make some coffee and grabbed the wrong can. When opened, out came a whole bunch of baby king snakes. She does not mind snakes, but she just wasn't expecting them. She even caught a large diamondback rattlesnake by herself that she found crossing the road while driving to town one time. She had to chase a guy off that wanted to kill it for her. She said he accused her of being crazy.

She was 75-years old at the time. They probably do not make moms like Ellen anymore.

Allen

My long-time friend Allen Uppon was down visiting from Canada. Allen used to help us at our shows in the Maritimes. I have known Allen and his family since he was a kid.

I had a very tame seven-foot alligator in our pond in the back yard. I raised Alley from a baby and he never bit anybody.

Anyway, I was feeding our big cats lions, tigers, and cougars. We had up to 35 cats at one time. I had 80 pounds of raw chicken in a wheelbarrow and whenever I went by the pond, I would give a few pieces to the gator.

Well this time, Allen said, "Let me feed the alligator."

I gave him a few chicken legs. The pond was over 20 feet deep with steep sides. It was dug for road fill before we bought the property.

Allen went to the edge of the pond and I called the gator over. He always came when I called, and he would eat a couple of pieces every day by taking them out of my hand. Alley came up to the edge and Allen leaned out with the meat. Suddenly the edge of the bank gave way and Allen fell right on top of the gator. It was amazing!

Allen catapulted out so fast, he almost didn't get wet. I never saw anyone move so fast and it scared poor Alley half to death.

Allen always had a knack for being in the wrong place at the wrong time. Just a few days after the above excitement, we were rattlesnake hunting along an old railroad bed. Allen was walking behind me since he wasn't too fond of rattlesnakes. There aren't too many in his part of Canada.

I scrambled down along the side of the roadbed to look in a hole and Allen continued by me down the track. I returned to the roadbed and Allen was about 20 feet ahead of me. I took a couple of steps and stopped.

"What was the matter with this one?" I asked Allen.

"What one?" he said.

I said, "This rattlesnake right here!"

He had walked right over a five-foot diamondback and never saw it. It was a good thing it wasn't a mad one. Allen was a little green for a while and he never walked in front of me again.

Every Day Is Different

One nice fall day I went road cruising up to Lehigh Acres, a vast housing development now, but very sparsely settled at the time. In the outskirts, there might be one house every mile or two. There were miles and miles of roads, more or less set up in a checkerboard pattern. You could never drive on every road in a day. There were all types of terrain there, swamps, high oaks, pines, and lots of palmettos full of gopher holes. The holes held tortoises and diamondbacks.

I drove around for a couple of hours and came up with five nice rattlesnakes. A couple were over five feet. They finally stopped crawling when it got a little warm. So I headed back home, about 40 miles away.

Weather-wise the next day was a carbon copy of the day before and I was looking forward to another day of catching some more rattlers. I drove around in basically the same area, plus a few places I did not cruise the day before. On this day I didn't see any diamondbacks, but I did find five hognose snakes. I do not think I have caught a hognose in Florida since. It is always fun to catch something different now and then, even if I did not find what I was really looking for

I did have one little distraction that made the day memorable. As I was driving around, I came upon a house way out by itself. It was amazing how many rattlesnakes I caught right by houses, much to most people's relief. Anyway, the house was pretty shaded and there was a station wagon parked along the road in the sun.

As I got nearer, I saw there was a young lady catching a few rays on top of the car in a bathing suit. Apparently, she had the top undone to avoid tan lines because as I drove by slowly, she sat up, but her top did not. I got all the way past before she realized what had happened. I just waved but it kind of made my day.

Dangerous Deer

As you know by now, my parents and I used to raise all kinds of animals: lions, tigers, cougars, bears, wild turkeys, leopards, deer, etc. This made for many interesting events. I remember one night three small fawns sleeping on the bed with me during one of our minor hurricanes. I guess they did not like the noise, but neither did I.

About ten years ago, I was down home in Immokalee, Florida moving some animals into different cages for my father. I wanted to put the deer into one of the old filming areas that was overgrown. The deer could browse and open it up in a hurry and give the grass in their pen time to grow back.

My wife Sandy was the only one around at the time, so we made a short tunnel with some wire panels between the two pens and opened the gates. Now deer get weird at times and this was one of those times. They did not want to go into the new pen, I went in to push them out.

Bucky was three years old and he only had four points, antlers, but he was one 150-pounds and tough at times. The two does were no trouble. I picked up a wire gate as a shield just to be on the safe side and it was a good thing I did. The two does went right in once I got behind them, but I had to push Bucky along every inch of the way. Finally, all three were in the new pen, and I shut the gate.

There were lots of vines in the new pen and Bucky nibbled on a few until he decided to fight with the vines. It ended up that he got his antlers tangled up in the vines and could not get loose. He was thrashing around so much, I thought he would break his neck. I took out my knife and went in to cut him loose. Well, with just a couple of swipes with my knife, I cut him free, but he was not grateful at all. Instead he turned around and charged me.

It was a good thing I had the gate. I put my foot against the bottom of the gate and my hand at the top. The standoff was pretty even for a while. He could not push me down and I could not push him back. I was up against two small trees so he could not get behind me, but he kept trying to go by going left and right. I thought I would just stay there for a while until he got tired. Then I could get out, but I was getting tired and he was still going strong.

He would back up, charge, and almost lift me off the ground. He could get more power because he had four feet on the ground. I really do not know why his antlers did not break. I got a little worried and I told Sandy to go find some help. She took off and I was now alone.

I still had the knife in my hand, and I was thinking that if he got through to me, I was going to have to cut his throat or something just as drastic. Just as I thought of that course of action, he threw up his head and knocked the knife out of my hand. I did not find it until a week later 20-feet away.

Now I was really worried, but luckily Sandy arrived with some help just then. They made enough noise to distract Bucky. At last I could get out of the pen. I came close to having some major holes in me.

A buddy of mine had the same thing happen to him and he was torn up pretty badly and in the hospital for two weeks. He now has two belly buttons.

Many people have been killed by their deer. I think I will stick mostly to snakes. They are a little easier to figure out.

Good Boy and Company

I have known a few people who have had dogs that would find snakes, but I have never had one. In Connecticut, when I was a kid, we had an English Pointer that would point snakes whenever she came upon one.

We had won many field trials for birds with her and she would make a very stylish point, head down, front foot curled up and tail held high. When it was a snake, she would wag her tail. Most of the time, it would be a black racer and it would take off. Several times, I found a nice hognose snake, usually playing dead about a foot away from her nose. I am glad she died of old age before we moved to Florida. She would not have lasted long standing a foot away from a diamondback rattler. We never had any dogs bitten in Connecticut although there are timber rattlesnakes and copperheads there. In Florida, we had several dogs bitten by cottonmouths and pigmy rattlesnakes, but none died.

Several years ago, I was driving down to see my parents and I noticed a small puppy along the road. He was just a little brown mutt about seven weeks old. I stopped to check on him since he was out in the middle of nowhere. However, he took off into the thick brush and I could not find him.

The next weekend I went by the same place and he was still there. This time he was so weak he could not get away. He was just skin and bones, wormy and mangy. My wife said we could not leave him there to die, and I had already made up my mind to keep him anyway. He had a lot of spunk - he needed it.

We got him cleaned up, some food in him, and he settled right in. A few days later, we took him to the vet. He had just about everything he could catch - three kinds of worms, mange, scabies, plus ticks, and fleas. We had a substantial vet bill, but my boss's wife felt sorry for the dog and helped us out.

He turned out to be a beautiful dog. My wife taught him several tricks and in one day he was totally house broken. Every time he did something right, we would say that's a good boy, so we just called him "Good Boy." Soon, he weighed 80 pounds. I was hoping to make him a snake hunter to help me hunt. I could see them, and he could smell them. I did not want him getting too close to them, so I took a feisty yellow rat snake I had, put it on the floor, and called him over.

He kind of smelled around it a little and it bit him on the nose. He has never gotten close to a snake since. He does not really hunt them, but if he comes across one, he just stands back and barks for me. He also circles around it if it tries to crawl away.

One humorous event happened with Good Boy. He often used to go to work with me at the tree farm. My boss had several dogs of his own and all the dogs got along. Good Boy's best buddy was Happy, a mutt about his own size. One day they were hanging around as I was working. I was right by the driveway when Anne Smith, the housekeeper, drove by. We worked together at times on projects in the house. She stopped to talk about something and the two dogs came over to say hello. All of a sudden, their ears went up and they took off into a shallow ditch near us grabbing at something. Then a big black and white tail popped up.

A skunk, I thought. Anne grabbed Happy by the collar and I got Good Boy. I did not relish driving home with a smelly dog and Sandy would have never let him in the house. The skunk started moving in the bushes and Happy slipped his collar and went after it again. Good Boy half dragged me in also.

Anne grabbed Happy by the tail, which only slowed him down a little. Then the skunk came out of the bushes and it was the biggest black and white fox squirrel I had ever seen. It tried to climb a queen palm tree, but the tree was so smooth its claws could not dig in very good. It got about four feet up and ran out of gas. Good Boy and Happy were snapping at its tail, so with my free hand, I kind of goosed it up into the fronds where it was out of danger. Anne and I sat on the ground and laughed for five minutes. Good Boy would chase anything that ran except a snake. Although he never caught much, he was a good boy.

Turner River Road

When we moved out to Immokalee from Davie, Florida I was only about five miles from the Turner River Road (TRR). It was one of my favorite places to road hunt and now it was 60 miles closer to my new home.

State Road 29 was parallel to Turner River Road and five miles apart. I would hunt along 29 until almost dark, then cut over to TRR and ride back and forth until I got tired or the snakes stopped crawling. TRR was a wide white dirt road, it still is, and there was very little traffic and almost no houses. The State was buying out everyone in the area and returning it to its natural state. They have even filled in some of the canal that ran parallel to the road so the water would flow back. I was living there before all this took place, however.

When I lived in Davie, I did not go all the way out there too often. I only went if the snakes were crawling good. After we moved out there, I would go out almost every evening during the warm parts of the year.

There were not a whole lot of good snakes, but there were a lot of snakes. The few good ones - kings and rats - kept it interesting. Rainy nights were not good as the road turned to grease. You had to stay in the middle of the road or you could end up in the canal.

Sometimes when it was dry, the road got a wash-board effect. It would get so bumpy you could hardly stay on the road and it would shake your teeth loose. The smaller snakes also got in the ruts and were hard to see. After writing this, I wonder why I liked it there so much.

Well, on the good evenings, you would get tired getting in and out of the car picking up snakes. A slow night was 20 or 30 snakes, but I have caught around 75 to 100 snakes numerous times. Most of them were garters, ribbons, and water snakes, but you always got a few reds and yellows, pigmy rattlesnakes, and cottonmouths. Before dark, you might get a diamondback now and then. The eastern diamondbacks very seldom crawl after dark, while the western diamondbacks crawl night or day, depending on the temperature.

Nothing was worth much in those days but even though at a dime or a quarter, it was enough of something to do. One of the dealers I sold to would take everything except very small pigmy rattlers. He would only take ten at a time, he was paying fifteen cents each in those days. Now they are worth 100 times that or more.

We would start out, catch our ten pigmy rattlers then bypass the rest. The next time out we would catch ten more. I used to take a lot of kids out there just to show them a good time. They would really get excited with so many snakes. I just had to watch and make sure they did not try to catch anything poisonous. I had my god-niece Diana out one time when she was about seven and she still talks about it. The road was about 20 miles long, between 1-75 and US 41 aka Alligator Alley. You never knew what you would catch. I remember one night, I caught a large coral snake, a scarlet king snake and a scarlet snake all on one run. That was the only time I ever caught the three tri-colors on the same drive.

All good things must end they say. Now, that whole area is in a wildlife management area with no snake hunting allowed although the deer hunters can still hunt there. They now have guided tours up and down the road. I hear it is quite popular, but I prefer to remember it as it was. I have not been down it in years.

Snakes Are Where You Find Them

Just the other night I was out riding the roads looking for red rat snakes. I finally found one, a nice four-footer but then a half hour passed without anything and I headed for home. I was just about out of the good area when I saw my buddy Bruce Beddner up ahead on his motorcycle.

He was stopped at the crossroad in front of me and he was picking up a snake. Bruce was tailing it, picking it up by the tail, so I knew it was a poisonous species. I pulled up close so he could use my headlights to see better since motorcycle lights are not that good. About the time I got out of the car to help, he got the coral snake in the bag. I stayed in the car and Bruce came over and we talked for a few minutes. He had also caught a single red rat. Bruce and I were sitting with my headlights on right in the middle of the road talking.

The houses had not been built yet that would go with this maze of roads. I glanced over Bruce's shoulder and there on the road about 30 feet away was a red rat snake crawling toward us.

I said, "Don't look now but there is a red rat snake that wants to be caught. It's crawling up to us."

Bruce said, "What, where?"

I said, "Over there."

He went over and picked it up. I did not even have to get out of the car. We split the money for the snake and away we went. It was the easiest half snake I ever caught.

Waltzing Bear

My wife and I were driving home from a visit to my mother's in Immokalee when I saw something big and black up ahead in the middle of the road. When I got close, I saw it was a big black bear that had been hit by a car. A Corvette had hit it I found out later. I pulled over on the shoulder and another car stopped on the other side at the same time. The guy that had hit the bear kept on going. We stopped traffic from both directions and the other guy had a cell phone and called the game department.

We walked over to the 300 to 400-pound bear and the guy said, "It's breathing!"

I said, "Yeah, we had better get it off the road. Maybe they can treat it, but I don't give it much hope!?"

I got it by the leg and pulled but nothing happened. It was like it was made of lead. The other guy tried to pull a little, but he was afraid and did not try very hard. No one else volunteered. Maybe they were smarter than us.

Well, I had to get it off the road, so I got two hands on his leg and gave a good pull and the bear sat up and looked at me. I backed up a little, then I poked him a little and told him to get up as he was too heavy to move. With that, he got up and started walking in circles. He had been knocked cold and was a little dizzy. The circles got bigger and bigger and were finally encompassing the whole road.

There was a canal right along the road with a guardrail. My helpmate said not to let him get over the guardrail as he might fall into the canal and drown. Yeah, like I was going to stop him. My wife Sandy was hollering at me to keep away from the bear. The bear did not really know I was there and I was close enough to the guardrail to jump over if l had to.

Finally, the bear came to the guardrail and remembered where he was, jumped over it, and rolled down into the canal. He came out and was walking along the edge. Then he swam over to the other side, about 25-feet, and went into the woods looking as good as new. There wasn't anything else we could do, so we continued on home having done our good deed for the day.

A few days later, I talked to one of the Fish and Game guys and he said that they had found the bear the next day asleep in a clump of palmettos not too far away. They also thought he looked as good as new, but the Corvette wasn't as lucky. The only low point of this affair was that my wife is a professional photographer, but she did not have her camera with her. She missed some pictures of a lifetime, me waltzing with a bear.

Alley the Gator

When we moved out to Immokalee back in the 1970's, I still had a few of the small gators left from the 28 we traded for the seven-foot croc from Jamaica. I turned them loose in the large rock pit that was on our property. This pond was a third of our five- acre lot, crystal clear and 20 feet deep. Only one of these gators stayed, and he was very tame. He would come any time I called him. He would eat out of my hand and never tried to bite me. He started off eating chicken necks and leftover cat food but grew up to eat whole chickens and road-kill opossums, raccoons, and squirrels. Gators are kind of a garbage can with legs and can swim.

I remember one year he came to eat every day, even on the days we had frost. The water didn't get below 60 degrees. We built a floating dock in this 50 by 300-foot pond and I would sit with my feet in the water. When Alley swam, I could grab his tail, and he would pull me off into the water. It looked pretty neat. He liked being tickled under his chin and I think he liked the attention.

We used him in many TV shows and a few movies. The only thing that got him upset were the other gators in the neighborhood. We lived way out in the middle of nowhere surrounded by wildlife. Once in a while a wild gator would come into the pond and Alley would chase the males away while allowing the females to stay awhile.

Alley got to be about eight feet and started bellowing with a male across the road in the canal. He finally went over to the canal and was gone for a couple of weeks. I went out to the mailbox one day and heard a noise in the canal. I went over and there was Alley by the bank with a hole in his side and a loop of intestines sticking out. I knew that I couldn't get a rope on him without hurting him more. The canal bank was pretty steep and there was a guardrail, too.

I could never lift him over it as he was over 200 pounds and I didn't have any help. Now, I'm no Dr. Doolittle, but I do talk to the animals, even snakes, and some of them seem to understand. Well, I told Alley to come back to our pond and I would fix him up. Would you believe the very next day, there he was lying on the bank in our yard. I washed the wound and slowly pushed his guts back in. They stayed in and healed up nicely. I often wondered what the other gator looked like.

A couple of years later, while I was off on a snake-hunting trip, Alley went wandering again and got hit by a pickup truck. He wrecked the truck, but no one was hurt except Alley. It took my father and another guy to roll him off the road. He did crawl into the canal, mostly by reflex I guess, because he never came home again. I still miss him he was a great gator.

A Few Fish Stories

My father swore you tame or train almost anything and I'm of the same thought.

When we moved to Immokalee, Florida, there was a large rock pit pond aka a borrow pit on the property. It is 50 by 300 feet and 20 feet deep with nice clear water allowing you to see the bottom in most places. I didn't get to check it out much until we got all the cat cages set up. I did take a swim now and then, however, to cool off. After we settled in, I was taking a walk along the edge of the pond when I noticed a largemouth bass following me. I used to do a lot of fishing, but I hadn't been in the mood lately.

As I walked along, I scared a frog into the water. The bass went over and grabbed it. A little further, another frog jumped in and the bass got that one too. I thought that was pretty neat and so did the bass. It followed me all the way around the pond, eating frogs as we went. The next day it was waiting for me and we did it again. When there weren't too many frogs, I'd catch anoles lizards for him. I guess the bass to be about two pounds at that time.

We used to feed chicken necks to our big cats — cougars, lions, tigers, leopards, and bobcats, plus sometimes wolves and bears. We could go through a 100 pounds of chicken a day.

There were always some leftovers that I'd feed to the alligator. If the gator missed a piece, I noticed that the bass would eat it.

Alley, the gator, would eat out of my hand. One day after the gator was full, the bass came over and took one out of my hand too. After that I couldn't get rid of the bass, he followed me whenever I came near the pond. Bass are very aggressive feeders. They don't suck stuff in like a goldfish. They come full speed, and sometimes it would get my fingers. Luckily their teeth are small, but blood was drawn sometimes.

I figured I should name it and the only fish name I could think of was Charlie Tuna, so Charlie it was. It wasn't big enough to be called Moby Dick. Charlie got a buddy for a while that only had one eye, so it was One-eyed Jack, but Jack disappeared after a couple of months.

A few years later a TV crew from Ft. Myers, Florida was doing a story on my father's cats. After they filmed the cat story, I was showing them around. They saw Charlie and wanted to do a story about me feeding him. To accommodate them, I thawed out a few smelt which Charlie loved. They got the camera set up and I went down to the edge of the pond. They said they were ready, and I held a fish about six inches above the water. Charlie exploded out of the water, took the fish, and my hand right up to the wrist. He hung there a second, then dropped back in the water. They took a few more feet of film and I thought they had some good shots. Charlie was a six pounder now. They showed it on the evening newscast, and it looked good. A few days later, I was watching the newscast and they said they were going to show the fish story again because so many people had written and/or called in about it. Some people, however, were saying that I held the fish and then dropped it and the news station ran the film backwards. Backwards, the film proved I didn't hold it. Lots of people used to come out to see Charlie and unless he was really full, he'd come over every time I swished my hand in the water.

One day, a guy from up north was out looking at our cats. I was showing him around, giving him the 25-cent tour. As we walked by the pond, he said he was a fisherman and asked what we did for bait down here. Well, I could see Charlie right there by the edge. I was feeling a little show-offish so I said, "No bait, we just put our hand in the water and grab the fish."

With that said, I put my hand in the water and Charlie grabbed my fingers. I closed my thumb on his jaw and lifted him out of the water. At six pounds, he was quite a handful. I showed him to the guy, then dropped him back in the pond. You know, that guy doesn't believe it yet.

I went out west snake hunting for almost two months and when I got back, I went down to the pond. At the edge, Charlie came shooting over, jumped out of the water, and did a flip. I think he remembered and had missed me for that was the only time I saw him do that

The next time I came back from a trip, Charlie was gone. Someone probably sneaked in and caught him, not that he was very hard to catch. He could also have been fighting with Alley over a piece of meat. Since Alley was over 200 pounds, it would have been no contest. I now have a new Charlie. He's about two pounds and growing fast. He acts just like the old Charlie, eating out of my hand and biting my fingers. He also has a little buddy about one pound, so I have a backup. I'm trying to teach him to jump through a hoop.

Watch your local TV, we may be on again.

Mouse in the Blouse

I was alone at our place in Immokalee. My parents were doing some shows in Canada for the summer. I was taking care of our big cats. We lived out in the middle of nowhere without neighbors. It was just as well because a lot of people don't like cougars and leopards living next door.

On this day, I looked out and saw a car stopped by our driveway. A young lady's car had broken down with a faulty gas line. It would take two days to fix it because we needed to get parts from Fort Lauderdale. I now had someone to talk to and since the cats and snakes are poor conversationalists, I felt lucky.

Krystyna was a very pretty young lady from Poland. We kept in touch after fixing the car. One day she called and said she had to drive from Palm Beach to Miami and wanted to meet me for lunch in Fort Lauderdale. Since I was going to sell some snakes and mice near there, lunch would work out fine. Besides, I would have been crazy to pass up a date with a beautiful girl. We agreed on a time and a restaurant. We arrived almost at the same time, went in, had a good meal and nice conversation.

Krystyna finally had to leave so we walked out to the cars where I showed her the snakes I was selling. She wasn't in to snakes much, but she happened to see the box of mice. When I had more mice than I needed for snake food, I would sell them to the snake dealers.

"Oh, how cute," she said. "Can I hold one?"

I took out a mouse and let her hold it. She related how as a little girl in Poland she never had any pets. I offered her one or even a snake, but she said she didn't have a place to keep them. I told her that mice get very friendly and are not much trouble. I related how I used to carry one around in my shirt pocket and it seemed to enjoy this. While saying this, I put the mouse in my shirt pocket, and it crawled around a little. Then it poked its head out and looked at her.

"How cute," she said. "Put it in my pocket!"

Well I started to, but there wasn't any room in her pocket. She insisted so I tried again. Well, the mouse didn't think much of this and ran up and down inside her blouse.

"Oh, that tickles," she giggled. She tried to catch it but couldn't and said for me to catch it.

There I was standing in the parking lot with my hands inside her blouse trying to capture a mouse. It was a very slippery mouse and we should have named it Speedy Gonzales. I would go left, the mouse would go right, and back and forth we went. I finally caught the lucky mouse and put it back in the box. I secretly thanked the mouse for its escapade. Then we both noticed everyone in the restaurant looking out the windows at us. You know, I bet they didn't even see the mouse. Just another one of life's embarrassing moments!

The Voice — My Guardian Angel

A few times in my life I've heard the "voice". My former wife Sandy says it is my Guardian Angel. I'm not sure what it is, but I've heard it.

There was a gopher tortoise hole a few miles from our house on a little sand rise near the highway. I often checked it out and sometimes caught a snake out sunning, usually a coachwhip. However, I hadn't caught anything there for about a year and I stopped looking.

I was driving into town one day when the voice in my head said, "Stop at the gopher hole!"

I replied to myself, "I don't want to stop. I haven't caught anything there in a long time!"

The voice said, "Stop anyway."

I said, "No!" to myself.

In truth, I felt kind of silly driving down the road arguing with myself. However, the car stopped by itself right next to the hole. Now, I figured as long as I was stopped, I had better look around the hole. There waiting for me was a seven-foot indigo and I caught it just before it escaped into the hole. I wonder if my guardian angel was awarded her wings for that good deed. I realize, there is no logical reason for this, but it did happen.

Another time, I heard the voice while snake hunting along Flamingo Road. It was at night and I was shining a light around the bases of dead trees. I was searching for scarlet king snakes in the debris underneath the trees. Then the voice said, "Look up in the tree."

I looked around, but there wasn't anyone there talking. I shined the light six feet up the tree and there was a 23-inch scarlet king just starting down a knothole. In another second or two, it would have been out of sight. I did catch it and it was the biggest scarlet king that I have ever caught, and I have caught hundreds of them. I guess it's not so bad hearing voices in your head.

Dinosaur Tracks and Fossilized Bones

I was in west Texas one day on roads new to me. I happened to see a small sign that said something about dinosaur tracks, and I decided to take a look. There was an A frame ladder to ease the climb over the barbed-wire fence and to keep people from stretching or breaking the fence in their desire to see the tracks.

It was low rolling country without much grass or bushes and very rocky. I walked around everywhere but I didn't see anything that looked like a dinosaur track. I was about to return when I saw the tracks. They were on a gentle slope and a recent rain had washed the dirt from them. There was still water in the tracks which made them stand out.

Without water, they would have been very hard to see. It was funny that the first impression I had was that the tracks were heading toward a low hill and I looked in that direction. I didn't want to come too close to the walking dinosaur even though I was 65 million years too late. I enjoyed this and photographed the tracks.

Just a few years ago, I was clearing some brush away from the road where I work. It was just a narrow dirt road leading up to the house and barn, but it was a mile long. The boss had recently applied another layer of shell rock to replenish the road after some heavy rains. I was always looking up and down the road for snakes because I have found a corn, yellow, and coral snake now and then.

Usually, I didn't pay much attention to what was under my feet. The shell rock fill came from a pit a few miles away but 30 miles from the gulf. In spite of this distance, the fill was loaded with seashells. I walked along thinking I might find a shark's tooth and I always liked stuff like that.

A recent rain had washed the sand and dirt off the bigger pieces of rock and shell. Suddenly, I realized a piece of rock was instead a piece of bone. Astonishingly, the more I looked, the more bones I found. They weren't dinosaur bones, but they were very old and from extinct animals and reptiles. I was finding lots of pieces of a giant tortoise, as big as a Volkswagen, horse teeth, camel teeth, wooly mammoth teeth, small turtle bones, rib and leg bones, and even pieces of petrified wood. None of my finds were spectacular, but they were fun to find and identify. I even found shell parts of a giant armadillo that had weighed as much as 400-500 pounds when alive.

Often after work, I walked the road looking for bones especially after a rain. The bones are all partially fossilized and in pretty good shape. The dead animals washed down the river into the bay where they rotted and sank to the bottom, then were covered up by seashells, and sand when the ocean receded.

And wouldn't you know it? I only found two small shark's teeth in a year of looking.

Sixth Sense

Many animals have senses we no longer have or know how to use. We had a leopard named Leah that was born at our place and we raised her in the house. She was very friendly for quite a while. She used to play King of the Hill with some of our house cats up in a large tree and she always won. Of course, she was a little bigger which helped.

We finally had to cage her when she started to wander. We didn't need any leopards running around the Big Cypress Swamp. A friend of ours, Allen Riggennan, a teacher at a high school in Miami, used to bring some students by on some of his nature hikes.

He came in one day with 20 kids to look at our big cats. This gave the kids a break from wading around in the swamp. As they came up to Leah's cage, her personality changed instantly. She jumped up on her high perch, started growling, and staring at one girl standing in the back. She looked right through everyone else and just stared at this one girl.

It turned out that this girl had a morbid fear of big cats and had all she could do to even stand there. She said she was too afraid to move, and the cat picked up on this. The leopard couldn't smell the girl because the wind was blowing the other way. I'm sure if the cat could have gotten out, she would have gone and tried to hurt the young girl.

We had a baby black bear that we also raised in the house. Our little house dog, which only weighed ten pounds, used to boss it around. If the bear started playing too roughly, the dog would bark and snap. The bear would then hide its head and calm down.

In a few years, the bear weighed 200 pounds and the dog was still ten. In spite of this, the dog could growl, and the bear would still hide its head. The bear thought the dog could still beat her up and the dog didn't know she couldn't.

All the big cats were interested in the smaller children that came by with their parents. They seemed to know that they should go after the smallest member of a group just like a cougar goes after the doe or fawn rather than jumping on the big antlered buck. I think animals clearly have a sixth sense.

ZZ TOP

That little old band from Texas. The phone rang one day. A guy said he heard that I caught rattlesnakes, and did I have any?

"Sure," I said. I'd been out the day before and had five nice big ones. He said he was the manager of a rock band and they used snakes and buzzards and other things in their stage show. Since their last snake had just died, they needed some more for their next show in a few days.

He said he could come right out if that was okay and I gave him directions. A little later, three guys came to the door. They were ZZ TOP, that little old band from Texas and one of my favorite groups. They bought all the snakes; plus, they had a baby gray fox they wanted to trade. I think I traded a snake for it. We named the fox ZZ and we had him for quite a while. He was a lot of fun.

We talked for a while. They were all sitting on the couch that was up against the wall. We had a large tame bobcat that lived loose with us and she slept with my parents. I had her shut up in a bedroom while I was bagging the snakes because she liked to tease the snakes.

The guys wanted to see Bobbi. What else would you call a bobcat?) I let her out. Bobcats are funny animals and they have a real sense of humor. She liked to play pool, at least she liked to knock the balls into the pockets. Anyway, she came out and walked around a while looking them over. They were still a little apprehensive at first about petting her. Bobbi finally went to the end of the couch and jumped up.

They were all wearing big cowboy hats, she walked along, and knocked all their hats off…bop, bop, bop. I actually thought I heard her laugh. After that they were okay with her.

They were nice guys who even gave me tickets to their show and a GREAT show it was. I even got to see my rattlesnakes again.

Diamondbacks and Pigmys

I like to catch any kind of snake, but when I find a diamondback, it's a whole different deal. I still get excited and shake for five minutes after I catch one. They really give me a thrill. If it didn't, it wouldn't be fun I suppose. I guess there is some danger involved and you can't let your guard down for an instant if you are smart.

Pigmy rattlesnakes don't get me very excited, but you have to be careful catching them. They seem to have a chip on their shoulders, if they had shoulders. They are wiggly little things that won't hang on a hook like a diamondback. If diamondbacks had attitudes like pigmys, they would be very hard to handle. You would even have a hard time getting close enough to pin one down, and I sure wouldn't try to tail one.

Pillstrom Tongs take most of the danger out of handling any poisonous snake. I don't pin poisonous ones anymore but just use the tongs or a hook. You still have to be careful where you walk.

Sometimes there are two or three diamondbacks together. So, if you see one, look around before you get too close. It's amazing how well even a large snake can blend into the ground cover. I once took a bunch of pictures of diamondbacks right where I found them before I caught them. Believe me, the ones that weren't in the open just couldn't be seen.

Pigmys at Dusk

My friend, John Kemnitzer from New York, was down recently and I wanted to take him to some of my old spots. I told him about a spot not too far from here where I used to find a lot of kings and he said, "Let's go." He's easy to get along with.

Walking along an old railroad bed we started finding pigmy rattlesnakes, no kings, just pigmys. We caught 19 of the little rattlers in less than an hour. We quit because it was almost dark, and we did not have any flashlights.

Years ago, you could go to one place and catch king snakes. Go to another place and catch reds or yellows and another place to find cottonmouths or rattlesnakes. Now, you catch what you find and not very many of them anymore.

Recent Happenings

These two events happened while I was writing this book. First, I was at work and eating my lunch in my car, I like to listen to the radio. I was looking out the window when I noticed a large coachwhip snake crawling by. Now coachwhips are hard to catch. They are fast, they bite, and they are not worth much. That being said, I still thought I would try and see if I could catch this one. I got out of my car slowly, walked within about five feet of it, and made a flying leap. Miraculously, I managed to grab the last six inches of its tail and it did not bite me.

I was already taking a few snakes down to sell at Glades Herps in Fort Myers the next day. I decided since I had it already, I would take it along it to pay for the gas.

When I arrived home, I had a message from an old buddy of mine. It seemed he needed a coachwhip badly and wanted to know if I could get him one. Usually, I catch a snake after I receive an order, not before. This was good news.

Another snake hunting buddy, John Kemnitzer, called from New York and asked if I had any yellow rat snakes. I said I had not found any in a few months. He said his old one had just died and to keep my eyes open for one. I had caught his snake many years ago.

"Sure," I said, "No need to buy one, if I can catch one!"

The very next day I drove to work, parked the car, got out and there five feet away was a nice four foot yellow. How's that for service? I also found another yellow that night just to make doubly sure.

One of our friends, Syd Chapin, also showed up that week and he hand delivered the snakes to John. Such service!

Watch Your Step

Recently, I went up to Gainesville, Florida to visit my brother Gary. It was only my second visit and I didn't know the area. One evening, I decided to drive around the neighborhood and look for likely places to find snakes. Gary sort of lived in the country but all the roads I drove on had too many houses. There were a few overgrown lots here and there. I didn't expect to find much, maybe a few rat snakes. I was mostly just exploring for future cruises. I was only a few blocks away from Gary's house when I came to a road that looked promising.

However, as I drove along, the number of houses increased. I decided to go to the road's end just in case it got wilder. By now, it was totally dark, and I had my headlights on. I approached two houses close together and there, in front, was a five-foot diamondback rattlesnake. I pulled to within 15 feet of it and sat for a few seconds staring at it.

I was completely surprised since I had never found a diamondback after dark except in Texas. I finally decided to catch the snake. Since I had not been expecting anything poisonous, my snake box was in the front of my capped pickup. I had to climb over everything for my box and I cut my hand grabbing my tongs. Finally, with the tongs I boxed it. The snake never rattled. I continued a short distance to the end of the road and turned around. Right where I had caught the rattlesnake less than five minutes before was a boy walking barefoot without a flashlight. Who knows? I might have saved his life. Never walk barefoot in poisonous snake country!

More About Frank Weed

To have Frank visit your school or organization with a live snake demonstration, email him at: flfrankweed@gmail.com. Frank also appreciates fan letters.

Frank at a Daytona book signing

www.ingramcontent.com/pod-product-compliance
Lightning Source LLC
LaVergne TN
LVHW051544070426
835507LV00021B/2390